MW00907893

Intermediate Social Studies A
U.S. History and Geography

Book 1: Beginnings to 1877

Michael Roessler

Lora Murphy

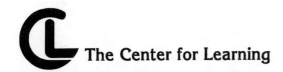

The Center for Learning

The Authors

Michael Roessler, who earned his Ph.D. at Michigan State University, teaches world geography and computer education. In addition to teaching part-time for the Teacher Education Department at MSU and serving as chairman of his school district's Social Studies Committee, he has developed ten social studies computer programs—three of which have won national awards.

Lora Murphy, who earned her M.A. at Case Western Reserve University, has been a junior/senior high school classroom teacher and department head, a K-12 social studies supervisor and consultant, and Project Director for the Center's *Basic Skills* series. She has studied social studies education in Australia and England as a Martha Holden Jennings Master Teacher and as a Fellow of the Rotary Scholarship for International Understanding.

Design and Illustration

Rose Schaffer, HM, M.A., President/Chief Executive Officer
Bernadette Vetter, HM, M.A., Vice President
Lora Murphy, M.A., Vice President, Social Studies Division
Diane Podnar, M.S., Production Director

Design and Illustration

Clare Parfitt

List of credits found on Acknowledgments page beginning on 190.

Copyright © 1992 The Center for Learning. Reprinted 1998.
Manufactured in the United States of America.

The worksheets in this book may be reproduced for academic purposes only and not for resale. Academic purposes refer to limited use within classroom and teaching settings only.

ISBN 1-56077-119-4

Contents

	Page	Handout
Cross Reference Chart		
Part I: Introductory Lesson		
1 Our Nation: An Introduction	1	1, 2, 3, 4, 5, 6, 7
Part II: History in General		
2 Attitudes Toward Social Studies	17	8, 9, 10
3 What if There Were No History?	25	11, 12
4 American Journey	29	13, 14
5 State Hangers	37	15, 16
Part III: People, Places, and Events		
6 Phillis Wheatley's Roles	47	17, 18
7 A Colonial Child's Day	55	19, 20
8 Biography—John Adams	65	21, 22
9 American History through Stamps	77	23, 24
10 Native American Acrostics	85	25, 26
11 Music of Slavery	95	27, 28
12 Name Origins	101	29, 30, 31, 32
13 McGuffey's Readers	113	33, 34
14 Family History	121	35, 36
15 Divide and Reunite	131	37, 38
Part IV: Geography		
16 Washington, D.C.	141	39, 40
17 The Local Area	149	41, 42
18 State Data	159	43, 44, 45
19 Climate	171	46, 47
20 Tornadoes	181	48, 49

Introduction

Intermediate Social Studies Activities: U.S. History and Geography, Book 1, Beginnings to 1877, is an interdisciplinary social studies curriculum unit for upper elementary and middle school students which has been developed around "hands-on" activities to promote student participation. Students are engaged in thinking, reading, writing, listening, researching, drawing, presenting, computing, taking notes, hypothesizing, singing, charting, graphing, comparing, contrasting, interpreting, generalizing, interviewing, and working with maps.

This unit is cross disciplinary as well as interdisciplinary. English/language arts, math, science, music, art, career education, health and safety, computer education, and home economics are interwoven with the organizing strand of social studies. In each lesson, the activity has been linked with specific social studies content from one of the social studies disciplines. As the title indicates, history and geography strands predominate, but economics, political science, sociology, and other areas of social studies are included.

These supplementary lessons are not ordered sequentially or arranged chronologically. The material in Part I has general application. Part II focuses on specific people, places, and events while Part III features geography topics.

This curriculum unit complements the graded courses of study, K-12 scope and sequence models, and frameworks developed by states and school districts. It is user friendly and designed to be easily adapted/tailored by the classroom teacher to meet student needs.

Teacher Notes

Cross Reference Chart

The plan and content of this curriculum unit are charted for easy teacher reference. The chart tells the teacher:

Lesson Title—Same heading that appears on contents page and at the beginning of the lesson

Featured Activities—Specific student functions

Topic—Subject which is the lesson's focus

Geographic Themes—NCGE's geographic themes from *Guidelines for Geographic Education: Elementary and Secondary Schools* which the lesson addresses

Objectives—Desired student outcomes

Skills—List of skills which the lesson reinforces

Interdisciplinary Strands—Disciplines involved other than social studies

Teacher Sections

The first pages of each lesson are written exclusively for the teacher. They contain the following information.

Objectives—Never more than three and always student-centered

Interdisciplinary Strands—Specific subject areas interwoven in the lesson

Notes to the Teacher—Background information and lesson overview

Materials—List of the items needed to teach the lesson as written

Terms—Vocabulary with which students need to be familiar

Sources—Some useful resources; check the local/school libraries for others

Procedures—A step by step suggested teaching approach

Extension/Enrichment—Optional activities for follow up

Student Materials

The last few pages of each lesson are activity sheets to be reproduced for students. They are of two types:

Samples—Examples provided for guidance; these pages are used to link the activity (designing a stamp) with specific social studies content (opening of the Erie Canal).

Handouts—Templates to be used for student work; these can be collected, kept in a portfolio, and later combined to form a student-written book.

Tips for Using the Unit

Student materials from the *introductory lesson* are useful throughout the year. Lessons assume that students have a knowledge base. The first lesson provides guidance for the basic research.

Directions are not given on the student handouts. Necessary instructions usually appear under the procedures in the teacher's section.

A *culminating product*—A resource book which is completely student-written material—is a viable option. The templates and section divider pages are designed to make this possible.

Each lesson is self-contained and designed to be *teacher-adapted*. The unit, in whole or part, can be adapted to whole language or traditional settings.

Suggested *assignments* provide both classwork and homework. Students are asked to complete activities outside of class time, but they are also provided with opportunities for classwork where the teacher and their peers are available as resources.

The use of the *library*—and other beyond-the-classroom resources (family, friends, neighborhood, community)—are integral parts of this unit.

There is a broad array of *skills* inherent in the lessons which range from lower level information retrieval to higher level decision making and critical thinking.

The unit lends itself to a *group work* format. Consider it as an option even in lessons where it is not specifically suggested.

The overall approach is *student-centered* and active rather than passive. The role of the teacher is to be a facilitator and guide . . . a supporting actor, not the star. Resist the temptation to be "overly helpful" and encourage students to help one another and themselves.

Cross Reference Chart (p. 1)

Lesson Title	Featured Activities	Topic	Geography Themes
1. Our Nation: An Introduction	Map Flag	Overview of U.S. in Time and Place	Location Place Human-Environment Interaction Regions
2. Attitudes Toward Social Studies	Survey Graph	Student Attitudes Toward Social Studies and Opinions about the Value of History	Location
3. What if There Were No History?	Cartoons	The Importance of History	Location
4. American Journey	Trip Itinerary	America's Historical Places	Location Place Movement Regions
5. State Hangers	Mobile Game	State History	Location
6. Phillis Wheatley's Roles	Role Clusters	Phillis Wheatley	Location Human-Environment Interaction
7. A Colonial Child's Day	Behavior Codes Daily Logs	Childhood in Colonial New England	Location Human-Environement Interaction Regions

Objectives	Skills	Interdisciplinary Strands
To develop a strategy for the study of the U.S. To integrate this basic knowledge with activities presented in the lessons and apply it to new situations including events both past and present	Reading Writing Researching Decision-Making	English/Language Arts Art Math Science Research Skills
To record student's initial attitudes toward U.S. history To study differing views of history To prepare a class profile graph	Reading Writing Graphing Decision-Making Critical Thinking	English/Language Arts Math
To understand the importance of history To interpret and draw cartoons	Writing Drawing	English/Language Arts Art
To plan a tour of the U.S. To learn about America's historic places	Reading Writing Researching Map Plotting	English/Language Arts Geography
To research state histories To learn about the people, places, and events of a selected state	Reading Writing Researching Drawing	English/Language Arts Art Geography
To understand social roles To compare oneself to one's parents and grandparents To learn about Phillis Wheatley	Reading Writing Researching Critical Thinking	English/Language Arts Geography
To understand the lives of children in colonial New England To compare/contrast one's life with that of a colonial child	Reading Writing Comparing/ Contrasting Critical Thinking	English/Language Arts Health Home Economics

Cross Reference Chart (p. 2)

Lesson Title	Featured Activities	Topic	Geography Themes
8. Biography—John Adams	Timeline	John Adams	Location Regions
9. American History through Stamps	Stamps	Benjamin Bannekar Opening of the Erie Canal	Location Place Human-Environment Interaction Movement Regions
10. Native American Acrostics	Acrostics	Tecumseh	Location Place Human-Environment Interaction Regions
11. Music of Slavery	Lyric Interpretation	Spirituals	Location
12. Name Origins	Charts	Ethnicity Martin Van Buren	Location Regions

Objectives	Skills	Interdisciplinary Strands
To read and evaluate a biography of an American To compare a famous American's life with one's own To learn about John Adams	Reading Writing Sequencing Researching Comparing/ Contrasting	English/Language Arts Career Education
To increase interest in U.S. history through exploration of U.S. postage stamps To learn about Benjamin Bannekar To understand the significance of the Erie Canal	Reading Writing Researching Drawing	English/Language Arts Art
To do research on famous native Americans To learn how to make an acrostic To learn about Tecumseh	Reading Writing Researching Drawing	English/Language Arts Art
To investigate slave songs of Antebellum America To explore music as social history in time and place To study the spiritual, "Go down, Moses"	Reading Writing Listening Researching Singing Critical Thinking	English/Language Arts Music
To develop awareness of ethnic origins To explore the origins of surnames To learn about the origins of Martin Van Buren's names	Reading Writing Researching Categorizing	English/Language Arts Art Geography

Cross Reference Chart (p. 3)

Lesson Title	Featured Activities	Topic	Geography Themes
13. McGuffey's Readers	Scholar's Slate	William Holmes McGuffey	Location
14. Family History	Autobiography Family Tree	Genealogy Abraham Lincoln	Location Regions
15. Divided and Reunited	Venn Diagrams	Sectionalism Civil War Reconstruction	Location Place Human-Environment Interaction Movement Regions
16. Washington, D.C.	Sketching Written and Oral Reports	Our Nation's Capital	Location Place Human-Environment Interaction Movement
17. Our Area	Map Graphic Presentation	The Local Area	Location Place Human-Environment Interaction Movement Regions

Objectives	Skills	Interdisciplinary Strands
To learn about William Holmes McGuffey To investigage McGuffey's Readers and their role in the teaching of morals To read and interpret poetry	Reading Writing Researching Constructing	English/Language Arts Art Career Education
To introduce genealogy To learn Abraham Lincoln's family history and understand its relationship to American history To encourage research into family history and investigage its relationship to American history	Reading Writing Researching Interviewing Charting	English/Language Arts Art Geography
To learn about the advantages and disadvantages of tne North and South during the Civil War era To practice using Venn diagrams to compare/contrast information and form hypotheses	Reading Note-Taking Categorizing Comparing Contrasting Hypothesizing	English/Language Arts Geography
To investigate the uniqueness of a national capital To learn about the capital of the United States, Washington, D.C.	Reading Writing Researching Presenting	English/Language Arts Art
To study the geography of the local area To understand the interrelationship of the local area, the region, the nation, and the world	Mapping Researching Computing Recording Reading Writing	English/Language Arts Art Geography Math Science

Cross Reference Chart (p. 4)

Lesson Title	Featured Activities	Topic	Geography Themes
18. State Data	Map Chart Game	Selected Data on the Fifty States	Location Place Human-Environment Interaction
19. Climate	Graphs	Climate in General and at Selected Locations	Location Place Human-Environment Interaction

20. Tornadoes	Map
	Chart
	Generalizing
		Tornado Statistics, Patterns, and Safety
		  Rules
			Location
			Place
			Human-Environment
			  Interaction
			Regions

Objectives	Skills	Interdisciplinary Strands
To learn about the states To evaluate the importance of different kinds of information To appreciate the uses of computers	Map Work Researching Recording Charting Gaming	Art Computer Education Geography Science
To read and interpret climate graphs To compare and contrast climates	Graphing Interpreting Researching	English/Language Arts Career Education Math Science
To understand the distribution of tornadoes To discern patterns of data displayed on a map To learn tornado safety rules	Map Work Interpreting Thinking Skills	English/Language Arts Art Geography Science Health and Safety

Part I

Introductory Lesson

Our Nation: An Introduction

Objectives

- To develop a strategy for study of the United States to include collecting data and identifying details about its history, geography, climate, government, economy, symbols, leaders, and other significant people, places, and events
- To integrate basic knowledge with activities in the lessons and apply it to new situations, including past and present events

Notes to the Teacher

The handouts in this lesson can serve either as an introduction to United States history and geography or can be adapted to continuing activities. The purpose of these handouts is to provide systematic experiences to help students acquire and practice research skills while establishing a knowledge base relative to a specific time period.

If used as an introduction, assign the present time, current data, and contemporary people, places, and events as lesson content to facilitate the research process with readily available information. Keep in mind that some school/local libraries may not have specialized resources containing information about some time periods which may result in the handouts being nonapplicable. The earlier in American history the era under study, the more likely handouts will not apply.

Alert students that responses often change over time. For instance, in 1810, the bordering countries were Great Britain, Russia, and Spain. By 1870 the bordering countries were Canada and Mexico.

Textbooks serving as the initial research resource can be supplemented by appropriate reference materials. Introduction will include good research techniques such as note taking rather than copying *directly* from source materials. Handouts permit students to practice writing research results *in their own words* which also assists the teacher in learning whether students synthesize reading materials.

After completing a study of the United States, the contents of this section and succeeding lessons can be put into book form to be bound and covered attractively and durably for use as resource material.

Interdisciplinary Strands

English/Language Arts, Art, Math, Science, Research Skills

MATERIALS:
Handouts 1–7, research materials, art supplies such as colored pencils, crayons, markers, scissors, construction paper, current newspapers, and magazines

TERMS:
culture, currency, economy, ethnicity, expectancy, literacy, per capita, precipitation, source

Procedure

1. Choose a time frame and determine how long to take for this series of handouts. Decide whether this is to be an individual exercise or a small group activity.

2. Explain that the first lesson dealing with the present day United States, will provide practice in research techniques and will familiarize students with handouts that will be used throughout the year.

3. Preview **Handout 1**. Introduce terms for students to define.

4. Explain what physical and/or political features are to be included on the map in **Handout 2** and instruct students in specific expectations for **Handout 3.**

5. Before students complete **Handout 4,** help them distinguish between important and famous. For example, rock stars, Graceland, and New Kids on the Block World Tour are famous. The President of the United States is important. Have students complete **Handouts 5 and 6** also and point out that the source category is for recording references from which material is obtained.

6. Review the examples in **Handout 7** to explain the process used in preparing a project bibliography. Then ask students to record references on bibliography cards referred to in the last paragraph of the handout.

7. Emphasize good research techniques and encourage rephrasing research into the student's own language.

8. A rough draft of research responses and edited material can be used both for peer and for teacher review. Use black felt tip pens which produce good photocopies, to prepare the final copy.

9. If a book is to culminate these lessons, duplicate the completed handouts to obtain two copies. This will provide students with one copy and leave one available as a classroom resource.

10. Establish portfolios and save each piece of the project in readiness for the culmination activity.

11. Create attractive covers using poster board or heavy paper that has been decorated.

12. Bind booklets either by sewing the pages together or by using a binding machine. A three-ring notebook also may be used.

Enrichment/Extension

1. Encourage students to illustrate the person, place and/or event selected for research.

2. Replicate the activity by studying the state and/or community in which the students live.

Social Studies Activities
U.S. History and Geography 1
Lesson 1
Handout 1 (page 1)

Name _____

Date _____

The United States Facts in_____

Location: _____

_____

Bordering Countries: _____

_____

Area: _____

*Rank in Size: _____

Population: _____

*Rank in Population: _____

Ethnic Groups by Percentage: _____

_____

_____

Major Language(s): _____

_____

Major Religions: _____

_____

Style of Government: _____

Current Government Leader: _____

Capital: _____

*Among countries of the world

© COPYRIGHT, The Center for Learning. Used with permission. Not for resale.

Name _____

Date _____

Major Cities: _____

_____

_____

Important Landforms and Waterforms: _____

_____

_____

Elevation: _____

Highest Point: _____

Lowest Point: _____

Natural Resources: _____

_____

_____

_____

Major Agricultural Products: _____

_____

_____

_____

Major Manufactured Products: _____

_____

_____

_____

    © COPYRIGHT, The Center for Learning. Used with permission. Not for resale.

Name _____

Date _____

Major Tourist Attractions: _____

Major Source of Employment: _____

Basic Unit of Currency: _____

Per Capita Income: _____

Transportation: _____

Communication—Numbers of . . .

    Televisions: _____

    Telephones: _____

    Radios: _____

    Daily Newspapers: _____

Life Expectancy: _____

Literacy Rate: _____

Current Problems/Current Advantages: _____

_____

_____

_____

_____

_____

Climate: _____

© COPYRIGHT, The Center for Learning. Used with permission. Not for resale.

Name _____

Date _____

Annual Precipitation: _____

Annual Temperature: _____

Types of Housing: _____

_____

_____

_____

_____

_____

Additional Interesting Facts: _____

_____

_____

_____

_____

_____

_____

Source(s): _____

_____

_____

© COPYRIGHT, The Center for Learning. Used with permission. Not for resale.

Social Studies Activities
U.S. History and Geography 1
Lesson 1
Handout 2

Name _____

Date _____

Geography: Map of the United States in _____

Legend

☐

Source: _____

_____

_____

© COPYRIGHT, The Center for Learning. Used with permission. Not for resale.

Name _____

Date _____

Flag of United States in _____

Source: _____

_____

_____

© COPYRIGHT, The Center for Learning. Used with permission. Not for resale.

Name _____

Date _____

An Important Person
in American History_____

Name: _____

Year of Birth: _____   Year of Death: _____

City, State/Country of Birth : _____

Brief Biography: _____

_____

_____

_____

_____

_____

_____

_____

_____

_____

_____

_____

_____

Source: _____

_____

_____

© COPYRIGHT, The Center for Learning. Used with permission. Not for resale.

Name _____

Date _____

An Important Place in
American History_____

Location: _____

_____

Physical Description: _____

_____

_____

_____

_____

Why This Place Is Important:_____

_____

_____

_____

_____

_____

_____

_____

Source: _____

_____

_____

© COPYRIGHT, The Center for Learning. Used with permission. Not for resale.

Name _____

Date _____

An Important Event in American History_____

What:_____

Where:_____

When (Month, Day, Year): _____

Who Was Involved:_____

_____

Importance to American History:_____

_____

Brief Description: _____

_____

_____

_____

_____

_____

_____

_____

Source:_____

_____

_____

_____

© COPYRIGHT, The Center for Learning. Used with permission. Not for resale.

Name _____

Date _____

How to Write a Bibliography

Books _____

Blackwood, Alan. Napoleon. New York: The Bookwright Press, 1987, 10.

   Author. Title (Underlined). Place of Publication:
   Publisher's Name, Copyright Year, Page Number(s).

Articles from magazines, newspaper, etc. _____

Vesilind, Priit J. "The Baltic: Arena of Power." National Geographic, May 1989, 602–
635.

   Author. Title of article. Title of publication. Date of Publication,
   Page Numbers.

Encyclopedia Articles _____

"Earthquake." Encyclopedia Americana. (Vol. 5), pp. 124–125.

   Title of article. Title of Encyclopedia. Vol. Number,
   Page Number(s).

Write each reference on 3" x 5" cards. When the project is complete, put the cards in
alphabetical order by the author's last name. Then, list them on paper in alphabetical
order with all the required information after the author's name.

© COPYRIGHT, The Center for Learning. Used with permission. Not for resale.

Part II

History in General

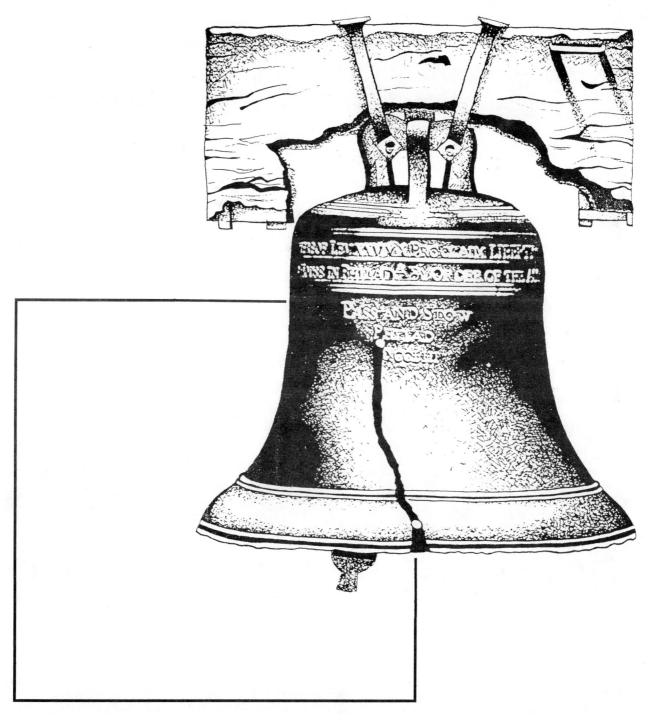

Attitudes Toward Social Studies

Objectives

- To record students' initial attitudes toward U.S. history
- To study differing views of history
- To prepare a graph which profiles the class's opinions about history

Interdisciplinary Strands

English/Language Arts, Math

Notes to the Teacher

When reviewing goals for teaching U.S. history, chances are that many of them consist of attitudes and values one hopes that students will acquire:

- To stimulate interest in history, politics, and current events;
- To increase the students' commitment to fundamental American values; and
- To increase tolerance for people who are different.

According to research on political socialization, elementary school is the best time for schools to influence the formation of these attitudes.[1]

The purpose of this lesson is to sensitize students to the importance of their feelings toward what they are studying. Administer this survey as the introductory activity before distributing the textbooks. Later, when students have completed their study of U.S. History, administer the survey again and have them compare and contrast attitudes toward history.

Don't be surprised if students' responses are not very positive toward social studies. Research has shown it to be a subject that they view as boring and unimportant.[2]

MATERIALS:
Handouts 8, 9, and 10

TERMS:
attitude, opinion, profile survey

Resources

1. Atwood, Virginia A. *Elementary Social Studies: Research as a Guide to Practice.* Washington, D.C., National Council for Social Studies, 1986.

---

[1] Walter C. Parker and Theodore Kaltsounis, "Citizenship and Law-Related Education," Virginia A. Atwood, Ed., *Elementary School Social Studies Research as a Guide to Practice* (Washington, D.C.: National Council for Social Studies, 1986), 14–33.

[2] Ibid. 5–6.

2. Gagnon, Paul, ed. *Historical Literacy: The Call for History in American Education.* New York: Macmillan Publishing Company, 1989.

3. Hoge, John D. and Claudin Crump. *Teaching History in the Elementary School.* Bloomington, Ind.: Social Studies Development Center, 1988.

Procedure

1. Introduce the terms. Tell students they are going to record some of their attitudes by completing a short survey. Indicate there are not "correct" and "incorrect" responses and that it is graded solely on participation. Encourage students to be candid.

2. Review the directions for **Handout 8.**

3. Have students complete the handout. Proctor to make sure that students put their Xs in the boxes and not on the lines. Remind students to respond to all of the items. Answers will vary.

4. Have students compare responses. Locate "interesting places" on a wall map. List the "Topics to Learn More About" on the chalkboard. Collect completed surveys and file for future use. At the end of the year when the survey is readministered, compare/contrast the initial and final survey results.

5. Conclude the initial survey by inviting student comments. As students share, listen carefully and use their comments to plan content and strategies.

6. Explain that people have differing views about what history is and what its value is. Discuss each quotation in **Handout 9** to clarify its meaning. Have students complete the activity. Answers will vary.

7. Debrief by sharing responses and reasons for the positions taken.

8. Tally class responses to each quotation on the chalkboard. Distribute **Handout 10**. Discuss group profiles and graphs. Have each student prepare a class profile graph.

9. Discuss the class profile as illustrated on student graphs. Remind students that even "experts" disagree on what history really is and how it is useful in helping us in the present and/or in predicting the future.

Enrichment/Extension

1. Have students do additional research and prepare lists of quotes indicating what history is and how it is useful. These can be printed on poster board and displayed in the classroom.

2. Solicit student opinions and learn their attitudes by having them prepare lists. Suggested categories: the five best American presidents; the three people from America's past I'd most like to have dinner with; if I could visit any three states in the U.S. I would go to . . . because . . ., and the five most important events in American history . . .

Name _____

Date _____

Survey of Attitudes Toward Social Studies

Directions: Read each statement carefully. Then put an X in the box that shows how you feel about that statement.

Sample:
Abraham Lincoln was a great president.

Strongly Disagree	Disagree	Neutral	Agree	Strongly Agree
				X

1. I am good at Social Studies.

Strongly Disagree	Disagree	Neutral	Agree	Strongly Agree

2. History dates confuse me.

Strongly Disagree	Disagree	Neutral	Agree	Strongly Agree

3. I like to hear stories about the past.

Strongly Disagree	Disagree	Neutral	Agree	Strongly Agree

4. I am interested in the news.

Strongly Disagree	Disagree	Neutral	Agree	Strongly Agree

5. I am good at reading maps.

Strongly Disagree	Disagree	Neutral	Agree	Strongly Agree

6. History is boring.

Strongly Disagree	Disagree	Neutral	Agree	Strongly Agree

© COPYRIGHT, The Center for Learning. Used with permission. Not for resale.

Name _____

Date _____

7. I am interested in my family's history.

Strongly Disagree	Disagree	Neutral	Agree	Strongly Agree

8. I get nervous when I take social studies tests.

Strongly Disagree	Disagree	Neutral	Agree	Strongly Agree

9. I like to read about the past.

Strongly Disagree	Disagree	Neutral	Agree	Strongly Agree

10. Knowing history is important.

Strongly Disagree	Disagree	Neutral	Agree	Strongly Agree

More Attitude Questions

The most interesting places in America are

1. _____

2. _____

3. _____

4. _____

History topics I would like to learn more about are

1. _____

2. _____

3. _____

4. _____

© COPYRIGHT, The Center for Learning. Used with permission. Not for resale.

Social Studies Activities
U.S. History and Geography 1
Lesson 2
Handout 9 (page 1)

Name _____

Date _____

Opinions About History

Directions: Read the following opinions about history. Think about each one. Decide if you agree or disagree. Circle your response. Use the space provided to tell *why* you agree or disagree with the statement.

1. "History is more or less bunk."[1]—*Henry Ford*
   I agree/disagree because

   _____

   _____

   _____

2. "The only thing new in the world is the history you don't know."[2]—*Harry S. Truman*
   I agree/disagree because

   _____

   _____

   _____

3. ". . . . we cannot escape history."[3]—*Abraham Lincoln*
   I agree/disagree because

   _____

   _____

   _____

4. "I know no way of judging of the future but by the past."[4]—*Patrick Henry*
   I agree/disagree because

   _____

   _____

   _____

[1] Bartlett, John, *Familiar Quotations,* Emily Morison Beck, Ed. (Boston: Little, Brown and Company, 1980), 587.

[2] Ibid., 788.

[3] Ibid., 522.

[4] Ibid., 383.

© COPYRIGHT, The Center for Learning. Used with permission. Not for resale.

Name _____

Date _____

5. "Those who cannot remember the past are condemned to repeat it."[5]—*George Santayana*
I agree/disagree because

_____

_____

_____

6. "Nothing changes more constantly than the past; for the past . . . does not consist of what actually happened, but of what men believe happened."[6]
—*Gerald White Johnson*
I agree/disagree because

_____

_____

_____

[5] Ibid., 703.

[6] Ibid., 816.

 © COPYRIGHT, The Center for Learning. Used with permission. Not for resale.

Name _____

Date _____

Class Profile

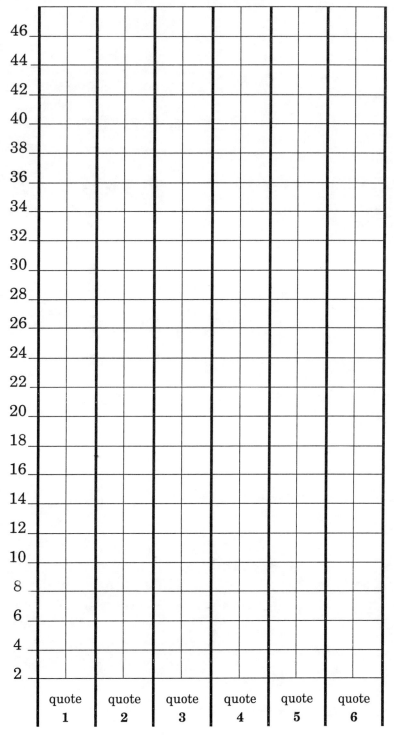

46
44
42
40
38
36
34
32
30
28
26
24
22
20
18
16
14
12
10
8
6
4
2

| quote 1 | quote 2 | quote 3 | quote 4 | quote 5 | quote 6 |

agree   disagree

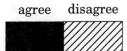

© COPYRIGHT, The Center for Learning. Used with permission. Not for resale.

What if There Were No History?

Objectives

- To understand the importance of history
- To work with cartoons

Interdisciplinary Strands

English/Language Arts, Art

Notes to the Teacher

Students often respond to a history lesson by whining, "Why do we have to study **THIS**? Although interested in the topics that collectively make up history, when considering history in the abstract, students may agree with Henry Ford's statement that "History is bunk."[1]

This lesson will respond to student's complaints and help them realize just how valuable history is. Use this lesson to stimulate discussion and its effects can be repeated throughout the year as students keep rediscovering new responses to the question—what if there were no history?

MATERIALS:
Handouts 11 and 12

TERMS:
alien, impish

Resources

1. Barr, Robert D., Barth, James L. and Shermis, S. Samuel. *Defining the Social Studies*. Washington, D.C.: NCSS, 1977.

2. Benjamin, Jules. *A Student's Guide to History*. New York: St. Martin's Press, 1975.

3. Bloch, Marc. *The Historian's Craft*. New York: Vintage Books, 1953.

4. Morrissett, Irving, ed. *Social Studies in the 80s*. Alexandria, Va.: ASCD, 1982.

Procedure

1. Engage students' imaginations by asking them this question: Suppose you were a playful alien visitor who wanted to confuse all the people on Earth. How would you do it?

---

[1] Laurence J. Peter, *Peter's Quotations: Ideas for Our Time* (New York: Bantam Books, Inc., 1977), 243.

Answers will vary. Let them spend two or three minutes suggesting possibilities (*e.g.*, change the labels on all canned goods, mix up the traffic lights).

2. Direct the discussion to the question posed in this lesson by asking: Suppose an impish alien destroyed all history books, historical records, and memories of the past. What would happen?

   Answers will vary. Have students share their responses.

3. When discussion lags, make a list on the chalkboard of some of the historical sources that would be lost:
   - biographies
   - constitutions
   - treaties
   - records of trials
   - birth, death, and marriage certificates
   - economic statistics
   - sports statistics
   - military records
   - family histories
   - ship logs

   Use this list to help students think of some additional consequences of eliminating history. Add these to the list.

4. Distribute **Handout 11**. Locate Mount Rushmore and Washington, D.C. Briefly discuss/debrief each cartoon. Be sure to point out that babies have no sense of history and must be taught "memory."

5. Have students complete **Handout 12**. Remind them that each bubble is to contain a question that people would be unable to answer without history. Let them share their ideas as they work; the exercise is more enjoyable if they feed on each other's insights. Each cartoon drawn should be different.

6. After students have completed their bubble questions and drawn their cartoons, have them share responses.
   Suggested Responses, **Handout 12:**
   Responses will vary, but might include the following:
   Isn't there a law against this? What's the world's record for this event? Has Canada been an enemy or friend of the U.S.? Where did my family come from? Why does she have an accent? Have prices ever gone up this fast before? Why are we such a rich country?

Enrichment/Extension

1. Assign students to watch a national newscast and record the number of ways that historical information is used. Discuss their findings in class the next day.

2. Invite a professional who uses history to visit the class and be interviewed by students. Newspaper reporters, newscasters, disc jockeys, politicians, lawyers, city planners, writers, and archivists are excellent choices for helping students reflect on the uses of history.

Social Studies Activities
U.S. History and Geography 1
Lesson 3
Handout 11—*Sample*

Name _____

Date _____

What if There Were No History?

Suppose an impish alien destroyed all the world's history books and everyone's memories of the past. What would happen? Show your answers by entering in each of the bubbles on **Handout 12** a question that people would be *unable* to answer without the help of history.

© COPYRIGHT, The Center for Learning. Used with permission. Not for resale.

Name _____

Date _____

What if There Were No History?

   © COPYRIGHT, The Center for Learning. Used with permission. Not for resale.

American Journey

Objectives

- To plan a tour of the United States
- To learn about America's historic places

Interdisciplinary Strands

English/Language Arts, Geography

Notes to the Teacher

This lesson uses U.S. history (historic places) and geography (their locations) to help students plan an itinerary for an imaginary trip. It provides an opportunity to review and reinforce cardinal and secondary directions.

Encourage students to be creative and establish their unique tour group rather than copy the one described at the beginning of **Handout 13**. If they have difficulty in sequencing their planned tour, help them avoid backtracking by locating and labeling all stops selected for **Handout 14**, page 1, before they begin the site descriptions. Most students have done connect-the-dots games, and using it as an analogy is helpful. If a longer trip is desired, reproduce additional copies of **Handout 14**, page 1, and renumber from 7 through 12. Help students develop a one or two sentence conclusion to their trips.

Films, slide programs, and videotapes of America's famous places can be shown for motivation and used to introduce this lesson. Resist the temptation to extend the introduction and keep it short—especially if using teacher-owned slides or videotapes.

MATERIALS:
Handouts 13 and 14, atlases, textbooks, reference books

TERMS:
historic, itinerary, sightseeing, tour

Resources

1. *America's Historic Places: An Illustrated Guide to Our Country's Past.* Pleasantville, NY: Reader's Digest Association, Inc., 1988.

2. Aylesworth, Thomas and Virginia L. Aylesworth. *America's National Parks.* New York: Bison Books Corp., 1984.

3. Harris, Bill. *America: The Fifty States.* New York: Crescent Books, 1985.

4. Cromie, Alice. *Restored Towns and Historic Districts of America: A Tour Guide.* New York: E.P. Dutton. 1979.

Procedure

1. Ask students to share places they have visited or know they would like to visit. Locate these on a wall map and/or globe.

2. Remind them that America has many places that are historically significant. Write the names of a dozen student-generated places important to our heritage on the chalkboard. Locate these on a wall map and add the appropriate location (state) of each one listed.

3. Introduce **Handout 13** as a clues game. Have students locate the first site on the map on **Handout 13,** page 3. Refer them to page 1, and indicate that to identify the site they must read the description, select a key word or phrase, look it up in the index, read the textbook page or reference section, and discover the name of the historic place visited.

4. Walk students through the first item as an example.

5. Have students, individually or in small groups, complete the activity. Review correct responses.
   Suggested Responses, Handout 13:

1. *Plymouth Rock*	7. *New Orleans*
2. *Fort Ticonderoga*	8. *St. Louis*
3. *Liberty Bell*	9. *The Alamo*
4. *Roanoke, Kitty Hawk*	10. *Sutter's Fort*
5. *Fort Sumter*	11. *Seattle*
6. *St. Augustine*	12. *Mt. Rushmore*

6. Encourage students to use the index of their textbooks and reference books to help plan their trip. Have them lay out their entire trip listing the six historic places selected on a separate piece of scrap paper as a beginning.

7. Proctor as students work on **Handout 14**. Provide help for those experiencing difficulty. Remind students that they are to place the numbers on their map correctly.

8. Have students become travel agents. Let them use a wall map to conduct their classmates on the trip they have planned.

Enrichment/Extension

1. Have students illustrate the historic places on their itinerary.

2. Use the sites selected as subjects for additional research and report topics.

3. Replicate the activity, and have students plan a world tour.

Social Studies Activities
U.S. History and Geography 1
Lesson 4
Handout 13 (page 1)—*Sample*

Name _____

Date _____

A Trip through American History

The travel agent knows that our family loves history and enjoys visiting historical sites. She has planned a coast-to-coast trip for us that is a history buff's delight as the following itinerary shows.

1. We begin our journey by visiting a spot made famous by the Pilgrims_____in Plymouth, Massachusetts. They left the *Mayflower* and landed here in 1620.

2. Leaving the shore, we travel to the mountains. We have come to see a place made famous by Ethan Allan and the Green Mountain Boys_____in Vermont.

3. We head southward and arrive in the City of Brotherly Love in Pennsylvania. We are in time to see both Independence Hall and the_____which the children were surprised to see is cracked.

4. Continuing south, we head again for the shore. On the outer banks of North Carolina we see not only the play, "The Lost Colony" at_____but climb the hill at—_____where the Wright brothers started their famous first flight.

5. The family seems to be in a rut because we are going south again. We went into South Carolina because we did not want to miss_____in the harbor of Charleston. The Civil War started when the Confederates fired on this Union fort.

6. This is getting ridiculous, but—you guessed it!—we are traveling south again. We couldn't resist going to Florida to see_____America's oldest city. The Spanish influence is clearly seen in the "old" part of town.

7. Finally we are not going south; we are headed west through the Florida Panhandle and Alabama to_____. It is a lovely city on the Mississippi River. Our hotel is located in

© COPYRIGHT, The Center for Learning. Used with permission. Not for resale.

Social Studies Activities
U.S. History and Geography 1
Lesson 4
Handout 13 (page 2)—*Sample*

Name _____

Date _____

the French Quarter and is so French that it almost makes us forget that Spain ruled here for many years.

8. We forsake auto travel and board a Mississippi riverboat. It takes us north up the Mississippi past Natchez and Vicksburg all the way to_____in Missouri. This city, known as Gateway to the West, is famous for its Arch which soars high above the riverfront. It is easy to imagine the wagon trains leaving for California and Oregon overland and flat boats loading up to float down river to the Gulf of Mexico.

9. From the banks of the Mississippi we travel by car southward to Texas. Milly is anxious to see_____in San Antonio. This is a popular tourist attraction despite the fact that Americans suffered a defeat at the hands of the Mexicans' army there.

10. The next stop on our trip is "way out West," as the song says. We cross the Rockies to get to_____outside of Sacramento. It is difficult to imagine that the California Gold Rush of 1849 started in this little settlement's sawmill on the American River.

11. We head for the coastal highway and travel north through Oregon into Washington. Our destination is that lovely city _____on Puget Sound. The Space Needle is fun for the whole family. The view of Mt. Rainier is spectacular from its revolving restaurant.

12. We leave Washington and head east toward the Black Hills of South Dakota. We all want to see the famous carved mountain_____with the four American presidents in bold relief. We take time to see the buffalo herd at Custer National Park which is nearby.

The next day we drive into Rapid City and fly home. The vacation trip is over, but it is one we'll remember for a long time.

   © COPYRIGHT, The Center for Learning. Used with permission. Not for resale.

Name _____

Date _____

A Tour Map of the United States

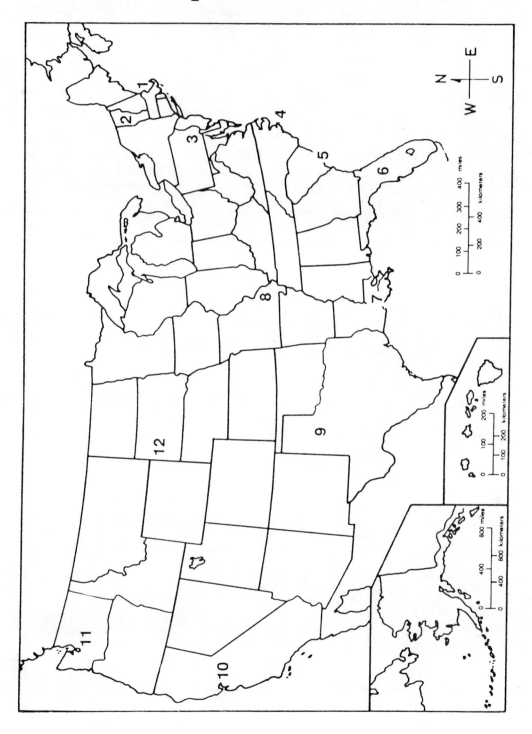

[1] *Merrill Social Studies: Outline Map Resource Book* (Columbus, Ohio: Charles E. Merrill Publishing Company, 1986), 6.

© COPYRIGHT, The Center for Learning. Used with permission. Not for resale.

Name _____

Date _____

My Trip through American History

_____

_____

_____

_____

1. _____

   _____

   _____

2. _____

   _____

   _____

3. _____

   _____

   _____

4. _____

   _____

   _____

5. _____

   _____

   _____

6. _____

   _____

   _____

© COPYRIGHT, The Center for Learning. Used with permission. Not for resale.

Name _____

Date _____

My Tour Map of the United States

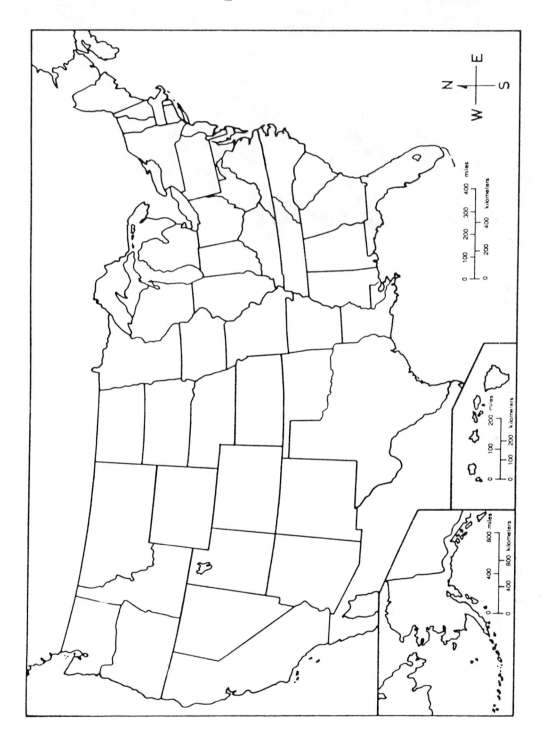

[2] Ibid.

© COPYRIGHT, The Center for Learning. Used with permission. Not for resale.

State Hangers

Objectives

- To research state histories
- To learn about the people, places, and events of a selected state

Interdisciplinary Strands

English/Language Arts, Art, Geography

Notes to the Teacher

This activity provides an opportunity for students to practice research skills, learn specific history/geography content, quiz each other in a game format, and prepare a classroom display.

Help students learn and practice the technique of shaping information into clue-type statements. Alert students to seek out a variety of information for their clue slips as they conduct their research. The clue slips should be varied—not all people's names or all dates, but a mix.

Remember to select colorful construction paper for the completed mobiles which is light enough to be read when written on with a felt-tip pen. Hangers can be personalized by wrapping them in yarn or spray painting them.

MATERIALS:
Handouts 15 and 16, encyclopedias, reference books, and art supplies—black felt-tip pens, colored markers, construction paper in various colors, scissors, a paper punch, yarn, wire clothes hangers

TERMS:
clue-type statement, factual statement

Resources

1. Andrews, Wayne, ed. *Concise Dictionary of American History*. New York: Charles Scribner's Sons, 1962.

2. Harris, Bill. *America: The Fifty States*. New York: Crescent Books, 1985.

3. Hoffman, Mark S., ed. *The World Almanac and Book of Facts 1990*. New York: Newspaper Enterprise Association, Inc., 1989.

4. Johnson, Thomas H. *The Oxford Companion to American History*. New York: Oxford University Press, 1976.

5. Morris, Richard B. *Encyclopedia of American History*. New York: Harper & Row, Publishers, 1961.

6. Schlesinger, Arthur M., Jr., ed. *The Almanac of American History*. New York: G.P. Putnam and Sons/Bison Books Corp., 1983.

Procedure

1. Utilize previously learned material about their state and have students make three factual statements that reflect its history and/or geography. List these on the chalkboard and help students turn the factual statements into clue-type statements. Repeat this procedure until students master the technique.

2. Instruct students to read each clue slip for handouts and record their response on the back.
   Suggested Responses, Handout 15:
   1. *Salem*
   2. *Cape Cod*
   3. *John and John Quincy Adams*
   4. *Plymouth Rock*
   5. *April 18, 1775*
   6. *Boston Tea Party*

3. Review correct responses. Locate the places. Ask students to identify the state, Massachusetts. Have students verbalize the connection between the illustrations and the information on the clue slips.

4. Have students select a state, research its history and geography, and prepare six clue statements with correct responses. Allow sufficient time and access to reference materials so students can complete the work. Check their clue statements and responses. This can be done as a class activity using a spell-down game format. Locate all correct responses on a wall map.

5. Distribute the art materials and **Handout 16**. (You will need two copies of the handout for each student.) Using **Handout 15** as an example, have students prepare their six clue slips. Have them make a seventh slip on white construction paper with their state's name on one side and student identification information on the other.

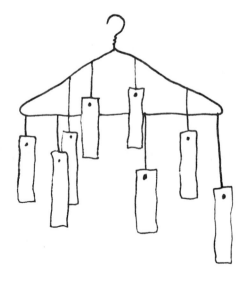

6. After the ends are punched, insert varying lengths of yarn and have students tie them to their clothes hangers to construct a mobile.
7. Use the hanger mobiles for classroom display.

Enrichment/Extension

1. Encourage students to read one another's mobiles. Use the information they contain for a spelldown-type review.

2. Replicate the activity using a variety of American history/geography topics—U.S. vice presidents, American rivers, state capitals, First Ladies.

3. Replicate the activity using global studies topics—leaders of countries, mountain ranges, river systems, famous events in World History.

4. Have students prepare the Introductory Lesson of this curriculum unit for the year in which their selected state attained statehood. States often entered the Union in groups, and this can be done as a small group activity based on the dates of entry into statehood.

Name _____

Date _____

A Colorful History

Infamous witch trials were held here in colonial times.

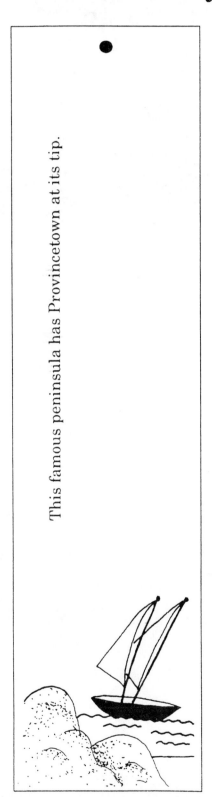

This famous peninsula has Provincetown at its tip.

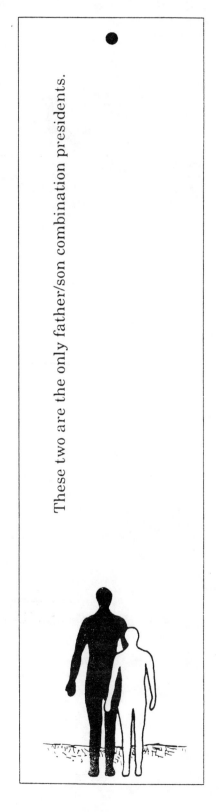

These two are the only father/son combination presidents.

© COPYRIGHT, The Center for Learning. Used with permission. Not for resale.

Name _____

Date _____

Every American's "pet rock"

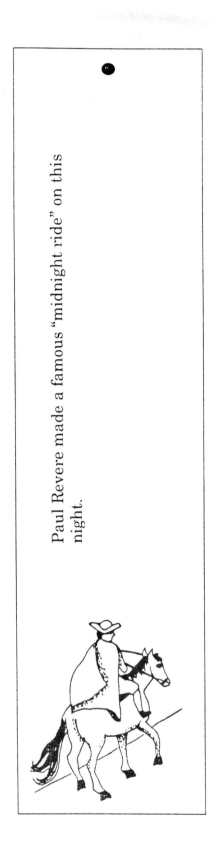

Paul Revere made a famous "midnight ride" on this night.

"Indians" dumped a famous cargo into our harbor at this festive event.

© COPYRIGHT, The Center for Learning. Used with permission. Not for resale.

Name _____

Date _____

My Colorful History

© COPYRIGHT, The Center for Learning. Used with permission. Not for resale.

Part III

People, Places, Events

Phillis Wheatley's Roles

Objectives

- To understand social roles
- To compare oneself to one's parents and grandparents
- To learn about Phillis Wheatley

Interdisciplinary Strands

English/Language Arts, Geography

Notes to the Teacher

This lesson investigates social roles and provides a way to record them. It gives students a biographical sketch of a famous American (Phillis Wheatley) and a sample roll cluster derived from that biography. It requires that students identify their social roles and those of a parent and a grandparent.

In a paper on how to teach family history, Dennis J. Thavenet demonstrates how a flower-shaped graphic can be used to display a person's many social roles. In this role cluster, one significant life role is written into each available space. By studying Phillis Wheatley's role cluster, by creating a cluster for themselves and then for members of two other generations of their family, students discover social changes that are embodied in their family's history.

Ideally, students complete this lesson by interviewing a parent and a grandparent. Some students will not have access to one or both of these relatives, and this is a matter to be handled with some delicacy. Make this assignment in such a way that these students will have other options and will not be embarrassed by their family situations. Give them the option of completing a role cluster by interviewing those familiar with the missing relative or by substituting someone of the same approximate age.

MATERIALS:
Handouts 17 and 18

TERMS:
biography, interview, oral history, role cluster, social history

Resources

1. Fritz, Jean. *What's the Big Idea, Ben Franklin?* New York: Coward McCann, Inc., 1976.

2. Joseph, Pamela B. "The Changing American Family," *Social Education,* October 1986, 458–463.

3. Thavenet, Dennis J. "Family History: Coming Face-to-Face with the Past," *How to Do It Series,* Series 2, No. 15, Washington D.C.: National Council for Social Studies, 1981.

Procedure

1. Ask students to give three one-word descriptions of themselves. Answers will vary, but words such as son, daughter, child, ball player, reader, etc. will be given. Select two students, and write their three descriptors on the chalkboard. Indicate that we all "wear many hats" or have more than one role in life.

2. Have students read **Handout 17,** page 1. Briefly discuss Phillis Wheatley's biography. Locate Boston and London on a wall map and a globe. Emphasize her role in early American history. Discuss why African Americans went to England and why discrimination was less of a problem there.

3. Distribute **Handout 17,** page 2, and remind students of the multi-role discussion held earlier. Have students, individually or in small groups review Phillis Wheatley's roles and study the role cluster diagram for her. Ask them to decide the two most important roles and underline them on the cluster diagram.

4. If more practice is needed in identifying roles:
   • Read a brief biography aloud—one of Jean Fritz's biographies would be ideal, particularly the one on Ben Franklin. Do a role cluster.

   • Read a section of the student textbook that discusses an individual in some detail—George Washington, Abagail Adams, Frederick Douglass—and do a role cluster.

   • If necessary, ask leading questions—What family roles did this person play? What occupational roles? Did this person have political or organizational roles? What did this person do for recreation?

5. Explain that role clusters can be used to learn about ourselves and our families. Using **Handout 18,** have students make a role cluster for themselves. Discuss the role clusters briefly. Have students underline the two roles they consider most important. Invite students to compare their clusters.

6. Distribute two additional copies of **Handout 18.** Ask students to prepare one role cluster for a parent or guardian and another for a grandparent (or for age-mates thereof). In order to complete this assignment, students have to conduct interviews with family members. Discuss this process with them. Have students list and record good questions to use in their interview. Remind them to ask the individual what roles are most important to them. Give them at least two days to complete the assignment.

7. When role clusters are completed, ask students to display results and allow time for viewing and sharing. Discuss their results. Use this discussion to tie broad social changes to the generational differences that students discover. For example, their cluster comparisons might reveal these trends:
   - an increase in the amount and importance of leisure time

   - a decrease in the amount and importance of household chores

   - a growing flexibility in the roles open to both sexes (*e.g.*, female working outside the home, women executives, male nurses, female body builders)

   - an increase in fitness activities (*e.g.*, jogging, running, "working out," walking)

   - a decrease in size of families

Enrichment/Extension

1. Have students illustrate the role clusters they have made by placing a small appropriate object in each sector. Have them color the sectors. Students may color code the sectors by type of role (*e.g.*, yellow for family roles, orange for economic roles).

2. Make role clusters for women and men from many different time periods in American history. Group these by historical periods and display them. Discuss the differences and possible reasons for the differences.

Social Studies Activities
U.S. History and Geography 1
Lesson 6
Handout 17 (page 1)

Name _____

Date _____

Phillis Wheatley

Phillis Wheatley was born in Senegal, Africa about 1753. She was bought at the Boston slave market eight years later by John Wheatley, a prosperous tailor who wanted a companion for his wife.

Mrs. Wheatley became very fond of the little slave girl she named Phillis. She taught her to read and write. As she grew older, Phillis found that the classic romantic poets were her favorite reading. Her favorite poet was Alexander Pope.

Phillis started to write poetry when she was thirteen. By 1773 she had written enough poems to have a collection of them published in London under the title, *Poems on Various Subjects*. She was in London, England, because her mistress had freed her the previous year and helped her secure passage to Europe. She became famous on both sides of the Atlantic Ocean as an accomplished poetess.

After her former masters, the Wheatleys, died, Phillis married a minister, John Peters. She bore him several children. She died in childbirth in 1784.

Thomas Jefferson did not like her poetry but George Washington did. People who wanted to end slavery pointed to Phillis as proof that Afro-Americans were capable, intelligent people.[1]

Source: Russell L. Adams, *Great Negroes Past and Present* (Chicago: Afro-Am Publishing Company, Inc., 1984), 148.

© COPYRIGHT, The Center for Learning. Used with permission. Not for resale.

Social Studies Activities
U.S. History and Geography 1
Lesson 6
Handout 17 (page 2)—*Sample*

Name _____

Date _____

Role Cluster

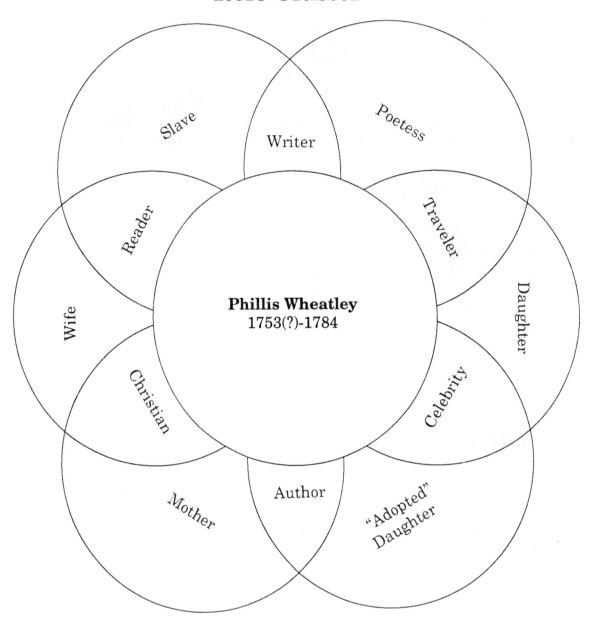

Slave

Writer

Poetess

Reader

Traveler

Wife

Phillis Wheatley
1753(?)-1784

Daughter

Christian

Celebrity

Mother

Author

"Adopted" Daughter

© COPYRIGHT, The Center for Learning. Used with permission. Not for resale.

Name _____

Date _____

Role Cluster

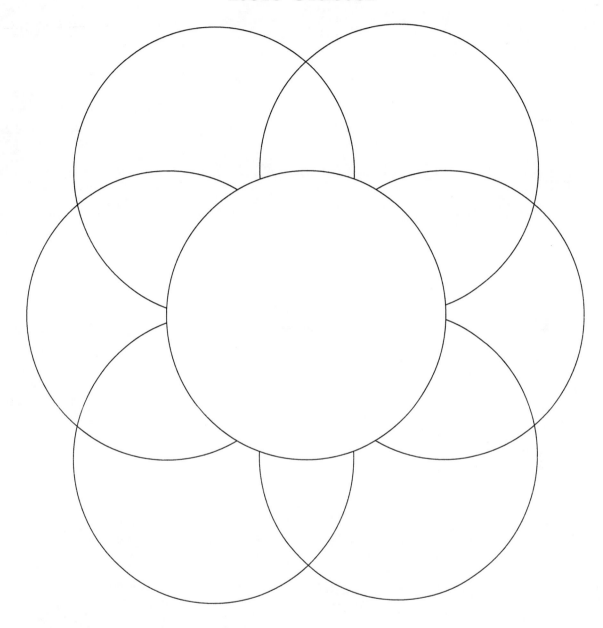

© COPYRIGHT, The Center for Learning. Used with permission. Not for resale.

A Colonial Child's Day

Objective

- To understand the lives of children in colonial New England
- To compare one's life with that of a colonial child

Interdisciplinary Strands

English/Language Arts, Health, Home Economics

Notes to the Teacher

Most history books write about the lives of adults. What were the children doing while our forefathers and foremothers were subduing this continent and building a mighty nation? This question is of interest to students. Helping them answer it makes them feel important. After all, if children 100 years ago were making history, it follows that children today are making history. Furthermore, the history of children is easiest for students to understand because it is one aspect of history which they can approach with a full experiential background.

1. This lesson provides an entry into childhood history through the use of two vehicles: daily logs and rules of behavior.

2. The roles provide a capsule view of the behavior code that colonial children were expected to abide by.

3. Two simulated logs are presented which are based on information contained in several books on the subject.

4. They enable students to learn about the daily life of children in colonial New England and compare it with theirs.

5. They show many aspects of colonial life through the typical experiences of colonial children. Decide if both logs are to be given to all students or if Anne's is to be distributed to the girls and Seth's to the boys.

These handouts will raise some specific questions about life in colonial New England. Why didn't Anne go to school? The sad truth is that 17th-century girls usually did not go to school. Most of the New England girls, at least, were taught how to read by their parents. After that, their education was mostly catch-as-catch-can. Occasionally, girls sat on the school steps and listened in on the boys' lessons. What they heard was usually something less than inspired pedagogy. Most schooling consisted of rote memory: copying and memorizing and reciting from memory.

These schools were not very well equipped. In fact, they were rather sparse. In winter, the heat, such as it was, emanated from a single fireplace. There was a teacher's desk and some benches and not much else. There were no maps and no chalkboards. Paper was very expensive and not available for student use. That's why Seth had to copy his arithmetic rules onto birch bark. However, there were some books available at school and at home. It is from some of them that **Handout 19** is derived.

Backboards were just one of several devices used to help colonial girls carry themselves erect. Stocks and harnesses were used for the same purpose. Also, girls wore stays, which were corsets made rigid by the insertion of wooden or metal busks.

Students may question the rules against smelling and inspecting one's meat. Due to the lack of refrigeration, colonial meat was quite redolent at times. Colonial adults and children preserved meat by salting, drying, and pickling.

In addition to these specifics, some general information about colonial children is helpful. Remind students that these young people were only allowed to be "children" for six or seven years. After that, they were expected to dress and work like their parents. Since girls had few career options, they worked with their mothers around the home: sewing, knitting, mending, carding, spinning, and doing a hundred other jobs that we take for granted today. Boys either went to school, worked with their fathers, or took an apprenticeship. Apprenticeships were often started by age fourteen and lasted for seven years. Apprentices lived with their masters and, occasionally, were allowed to visit their families. The age of majority was usually considered to be sixteen. At that age, boys could join the militia, and they were required to pay taxes. It was not unheard of for young people to marry around age sixteen; but, in his study of Plymouth, Massachusetts, John Demos found the average age of first marriages was around twenty-six for men and twenty for women. He also documented that Plymouth families were large: an average of over seven children born per family.

Concerning the all important question, "But what did they do for fun?," students might like to know that colonial children played many of the same games that they do: hopscotch, tag, marbles, dolls, cat's cradle, ball, and the ever-popular torment-your-brothers-and-sisters. Boys especially loved to hunt and fish, which they did for work and pleasure. [A child's favorite tool was the jackknife.] Colonial children had very few toys. The ones they had they usually made for themselves.

MATERIALS:
Handouts 19 and 20

TERMS:
backboard, ciphering, jerky, pewter, shucking, venison

Resources

1. Blos, Joan W. *A Gathering of Days: A New England Girl's Journal. 1830–32.* New York: Charles Scribner's Sons, 1979.

2. Cable, Mary. *The Little Darlings: A History of Child Rearing in America.* New York: Charles Scribner's Sons, 1975.

3. Demos, John. *A Little Commonwealth: Family Life in Plymouth.* London: Oxford University Press, Inc., 1970.

4. Downey, Matthew T., ed. "Children in the Making of History." Special issue of *Social Education,* (April/May, 1986).

5. Glubok, Shirley. *Home and Child Life in Colonial Days.* London: The Macmillan Company, 1969.

6. Kalman, Bobbie. *Early Village Life.* New York: Crabtree Publishing Company, 1981.

7. Knight, James E. *Adventures in Colonial America Series.* Mahwah, N.J.: Troll Associates, 1982.

8. Morgan, Edmund S. *The Puritan Family: Religion and Domestic Relations in Seventeenth-Century New England.* New York: Harper & Row Publishers, 1966.

9. Wright, Louis B. *Life in Colonial America.* New York: Capricorn Books, 1971.

Procedure

1. Ask students what they know about the lives of children in colonial America. List their impressions on the chalkboard.

2. Have students read the rules on **Handout 19.** Point out that these apply to New England. Locate New England on a wall map. Name and locate the Middle and Southern Colonies. Conduct a discussion which focuses on why the rules were as they were. Rule 1, for example, reflects the importance of religion in colonial New England. Rule 6 indicates that furniture, at least benches, was at a premium and that the entire family could not be seated at one time. Rule 12 speaks to the sanitary/health knowledge of that time.

3. Review the daily logs of **Handout 19.** After discussing each and reflecting on what it tells us about childhood in colonial days, compare/contrast them by gender. Help students speculate on the differences they discovered and possible reasons for them.

4. Ask students to use **Handout 20** to keep a similar log for a day for the sake of comparison. Remind them to include their meals.

5. Have students use **Handout 20** to make a list of rules of behavior that adults expect them to live by. This is an excellent small group activity. If students falter, ask them to think of rules that apply to different situations—going to school, working in the kitchen, preparing for bed, going to church, and other activities.

6. Debrief the daily logs and rules by sharing and identifying commonalities and unique features. Compare/contrast today's logs and rules with those of colonial children.

7. Review student lists of impressions from the beginning of the lesson. Help them categorize the lists as correct or incorrect.

8. Conclude the lesson by asking students whether they would rather be a young person in colonial days or today and why. Ask them to speculate how daily logs and behavior rules will look in 2090 A.D. Have them explain and defend their ideas.

Enrichment/Extension

1. Shirley Glubok summarized colonial children's knowledge of the world in this way:

   The child of colonial days had little knowledge at large. He probably had never seen a map of the world, and if he had, he didn't understand it. There was no foreign news in the present sense.[1]

   Discuss with students the extent to which this differs from modern children's knowledge of the world, if at all. What difference does it make? How aware were colonial adults of events occurring in the rest of their world or even in adjacent colonies?

2. Have students read about and create similar time logs for children living in other periods of American history.

3. Add a global dimension by having students read about and create similar time logs for children living in the Third World. Compare/contrast the time logs they create with a time log of their day.

4. Turn the classroom into a New England schoolhouse for a morning and teach the lessons as a school master did back then. Have students discuss education then and now.

---

[1] Shirley Glubok, *Home and Child Life in Colonial Day* (London: The Macmillan Company, 1969), 105–106.

Social Studies Activities
U.S. History and Geography 1
Lesson 7
Handout 19 (page 1)

Name _____

Date _____

Rules of Behavior for Colonial Children

1. Be not proud: "In Adam's fall we sinned all."

2. Keep busy. An idle mind is the Devil's workshop.

3. When an adult speaks to you, stand up. Never question what you are told and never say, "I've already heard that."

4. Don't run through the streets too hastily, nor too slowly. Don't make silly postures with your head, hands, feet, or body. Don't throw dirt or stones.

5. Girls should strive to sit and stand erectly. To this end, they should spend some time each day strapped to the backboard.

6. When called to eat, stand at the table so the adults can use the available benches.

7. Ask for nothing. Speak not, sing not, hum not, wiggle not.

8. Don't stuff your mouth so as to fill your cheeks. Be content with smaller mouthfuls.

9. Don't smell your meat or turn it round and round to inspect it.

10. Don't look earnestly at any other person that is eating.

11. When moderately satisfied, leave the table.

12. Spit nowhere in the room but in the corner.[1]

---

[1] These rules are based on quotations and descriptions provided in Shirley Glubok's *Home and Child Life in Colonial Days,* London: The Macmillan Company, 1969, 53 ff., 107 ff., 126 ff.

© COPYRIGHT, The Center for Learning. Used with permission. Not for resale.

Name _____

Date _____

Daily Log of a Colonial Girl

This log shows how a ten-year-old girl named Anne Henderson might have spent one day in November 1690.

5:15   Rise, dress, and help mother prepare breakfast of waffles and milk.

6:00   Eat quickly. Do chores of sweeping, cleaning, shining the pewter plates, and caring for the two younger children.

7:10   Run outside and join the fire-bucket brigade to save Widow Goodall's house. Dawdle afterward to chat with cousins.

8:20   Return to chores of mending clothes and spinning yarn.

10:45 Help mother prepare lunch of boiled beef, carrots, bread, and water.

11:30 Eat lunch. Feed the animals.

12:00 Work with parents to kill a pig. Separate the bristles from the hide. Empty and clean out the small intestines for sausage casings. Make blood pudding.

2:00   Take the bristles to the brush maker and exchange them for some fine blue ribbon. Pick up fire bucket from the fire warden on the way home.

4:00   Tend sister Hannah, who is ill. Knit some on a scarf for mother.

5:15   Eat dinner of sausage, pumpkin, bread, and blood pudding. Clean up. Read *Spiritual Milk for Babes.*

6:30   Go to cousins' house for corn shucking. While shucking, visit with friends and relatives. Join in singing and dancing afterward.

9:30   Walk home with parents, listen to Bible reading, and go to bed.

© COPYRIGHT, The Center for Learning. Used with permission. Not for resale.

Social Studies Activities
U.S. History and Geography 1
Lesson 7
Handout 19 (page 3)—*Sample*

Name _____

Date _____

Daily Log of a Colonial Boy

This log shows how Seth Johnson, an eleven-year-old Massachusetts boy, might have spent a winter's day in 1690.

5:30 Rise, dress quickly, and feed the fire in the fireplace. Bring in firewood and milk Josie, the cow.

6:30 Eat breakfast of toast and milk.

7:00 Walk to school early. Haul firewood.

8:00 School begins with lessons in spelling, reading, and penmanship. Grateful to be near the fire.

11:00 Return home, chased by older boys throwing snowballs.

11:30 Chop wood. Eat lunch of smoked cod, sweet potatoes, and cider. Help father make a chair.

12:35 Return to school. Confused by ciphering problems and rules copied onto birch bark. Receive stern lecture for not paying attention. Also for breaking quill point.

4:00 Run to old Johnson's hill for brief sledding adventure. Then run home for chores of broom-making and animal feeding.

5:45 Eat dinner of venison jerky, bread, apple pie, and cider.

6:30 Carry more firewood and help father with chair making.

7:15 Sit close to the fire with the family and shell corn. Listen to father read from the Bible.

8:30 Prepare bed with a warming pan and retire for the night.

© COPYRIGHT, The Center for Learning. Used with permission. Not for resale.

Name _____

Date _____

My Daily Log

Date _____

_____

_____

_____

_____

_____

_____

_____

_____

_____

_____

_____

_____

_____

_____

_____

_____

_____

_____

_____

_____

_____

_____

_____

_____

© COPYRIGHT, The Center for Learning. Used with permission. Not for resale.

Name _____

Date _____

My Daily Log (continued)

Date _____

_____

_____

_____

_____

_____

_____

_____

_____

_____

_____

_____

_____

_____

_____

_____

_____

_____

_____

_____

_____

_____

_____

_____

© COPYRIGHT, The Center for Learning. Used with permission. Not for resale.

Social Studies Activities
U.S. History and Geography 1
Lesson 7
Handout 20 (page 3)

Name _____

Date _____

Rules of Behavior for Today's Children

_____

_____

_____

_____

_____

_____

_____

_____

_____

_____

_____

_____

_____

_____

_____

_____

_____

_____

_____

_____

"How many times
do I have to tell you?"

_____

_____

_____

_____

_____

_____

© COPYRIGHT, The Center for Learning. Used with permission. Not for resale.

Biography: John Adams

Objective

- To read and evaluate a biography of an American
- To compare a famous American's life to one's own
- To learn about John Adams

Interdisciplinary Strands

English/Language Arts, Career Education, and other subjects depending on the biographies chosen

Notes to the Teacher

Students relate to history from a personal point of view. Biographies help young people connect with a person and better understand the past. This lesson provides a scaffolding around which to build a "Now-we're-going-to-read-a-biography" assignment. It reinforces interests and skills developed in other lessons.

The key to this activity is helping students choose good books to read. An annotated bibliography of the best biographies available in your school (and/or public) library is useful. If one is not available, ask the librarian for recommendations. Check *Social Education's* annual review of "Notable Children's Trade Books in the Social Studies."

This assignment is an obvious way to promote career education and provide role models for students with special needs and interests. Consult with other staff members about what biographies to recommend to different students: math and science teachers, gifted and talented coordinator, fine arts teachers, special education teachers, and others.

The handouts are designed to help students take notes while they read biographies and analyze the individual's life while they do so. Provide students one copy of the handouts on which to take notes and a second one for their final report. The timeline handout is challenging; it requires them to match information from their biography with factual content from their textbooks. Be prepared to provide assistance.

MATERIALS:
Handouts 21 and 22, collection of biographies, reference books

TERMS:
biography, career, values

Resources

1. Christ, Henry I. *American Biographies*. New York: Globe Book Company, 1987.

2. John A. Garraty. *1,001 Things Everyone Should Know About American History*. New York: Bantam, Doubleday, Dell Publishing Group, Inc., 1989.

3. Healy, Diana Dixon. *America's First Ladies: Private Lives of the Presidential Wives*. New York: Atheneum Macmillan Publishing Company, 1988.

4. "Notable 1988 Children's Trade Books in the Field of Social Studies," in *Social Education,* April/May, 1989, 233–240.

5. Odland, Norine. "American History in Fact and Fiction: Literature for Young Readers," in *Social Education* (October, 1980), 474–481.

6. Pope, John A. Jr., editor-in-chief. *Strange Stories, Amazing Facts of America's Past*. Pleasantville, N.Y.: Readers Digest Association, Inc., 1989.

7. Styler, Sandra. "A Selected List of Women's Biographies for the Social Studies," in *Social Education,* (Nov./Dec., 1984), 554–564.

8. Encyclopedia of Presidents Series by Children's Press (Regensteiner Publishing Enterprises, Inc.)

9. Any of the biographies by Jean Fritz

Procedure

1. Write the word "biography" on the chalkboard and teach students the meaning of its two parts. *Bio* means "life" and *graphy* means "a study of." Explain the difference between autobiography and biography.

2. Read **Handout 21**, page 1, aloud. Briefly discuss John Adams and his role in American history. Locate New England, Massachusetts, Washington, D.C., and Europe on a wall map. Note the source of the information. It is a biography of John Adams.

3. Use the timeline on page 2 of **Handout 21** to review the significant dates in John Adams's life. Call attention to the gaps—his teenage years when he was busy growing up and his later years when he had retired to his farm in Quincy, Massachusetts. Review the significant dates in American history. Compare the two sets of dates.

4. Discuss what is missing from the first two handouts. They are the factual approach. There is no analysis or evaluation—even by the person who is the subject of the biography. Look over the information asked for in pages 3 and 4 of **Handout 21** and contrast it with what was needed for pages 1 and 2. Be sure students see the subjective content asked for. Review what John Adams thought and the opinion of the nameless person whose evaluation is provided.

5. Explain that each student will read a biography of his or her choice, write a brief biography, construct a timeline, and prepare a subjective evaluation of the person selected as the subject for the assignment.

6. Provide enough time for students to complete all pages of **Handout 22**. Monitor as they read their biographies and take notes on the handout.

7. Distribute another copy of **Handout 22**. Have students complete the final version of their brief biographies, timelines, and evaluations.

8. Reap the rewards of student efforts by arranging for visual or oral sharing.

Enrichment/Extension

1. Have students don simple costumes and role-play the person they selected. They should be prepared to answer questions from the class on their person.

2. Have students research and write biographies of persons they know.

3. Provide a global perspective by having students replicate the assignment using persons from another country.

4. Present and discuss the following quote:
   "Men make history and not the other way around. In periods where there is no leadership, society stands still. Progress occurs when courageous, skillful leaders seize the opportunity to change things for the better."

   Harry S Truman[1]

   Be sure to note the gender discrimination in his statement. Cross out "men" and write in "people" before continuing with the discussion.

[1] Laurence J. Peter, *Peter's Quotations* (New York: Bantam Books, Inc., 1977), 243.

Name _____

Date _____

A Brief Biography: John Adams

John Adams was born in Quincy, Massachusetts, on October 30, 1735. He graduated from Harvard University. He studied law and became a lawyer.

He was active in politics and spoke out against the Stamp Act. He was a Patriot and was against the British. However, he defended the British soldiers in the Boston Massacre trial.

He served in the Continental Congress and was part of the committee that planned the Declaration of Independence. During the American Revolution, he was a diplomat and served in Europe. He was one of the signers of the Treaty of Paris that ended the war.

In the first presidential election the new nation held, John Adams came in second and became George Washington's vice president. In 1797 he became President. John and Abigail Adams were the first family to live in what is now The White House.

John Adams died on America's 50th birthday—on July 4, 1826. He was ninety years old and had lived to see his son, John Quincy Adams, become President.

Source: Marlene Targ Brill, *John Adams: Second President of the United States* (Chicago: Children's Press, 1986).

© COPYRIGHT, The Center for Learning. Used with permission. Not for resale.

Name _____

Date _____

Biography Timeline

JOHN ADAMS		AMERICAN HISTORY

1730

1733 Colony of Georgia founded

Born Oct. 30 1735

1740

1747 Ben Franklin publishes *Poor Richard's Almanack* in Philadelphia

1750

Attends Harvard 1751

1754 French and Indian War begins

1760

1763 England proclaims land beyond Alleghenies belongs to the Indians

Marries Abigail Smith 1764

1770

Lawyer for British in Boston Massacre Trial 1773

Helped write the Declaration of Independence 1776

1776 Declaration of Independence written

1780

Signed Peace Treaty 1783

1787 Constitutional Convention held

Became first Vice President 1789

1790

1794 Washington's second term begins

Elected President 1797

1800

Retires to Massachusetts 1801

1803 Louisiana Purchase

1810

1814 Battle of New Orleans

1820

Died on July 4 1826

1828 Andrew Jackson elected President

1830

© COPYRIGHT, The Center for Learning. Used with permission. Not for resale.

1826

Social Studies Activities
U.S. History and Geography 1
Lesson 8
Handout 21 (page 3)—*Sample*

Name _____

Date _____

Biography Views

Key Quotes: **John Adams**

"I am obnoxious, suspected, and unpopular."[1]

The vice presidency is ". . . the most insignificant office ever the invention of man."[2]

John Adams

Fascinating Facts:

1. John Adams defended the British soldiers charged with murder in the Boston Massacre.

2. John Adams lived to see his son become President of the U.S.

3. The two enemies—John Adams and Thomas Jefferson—both died on July 4, 1826.

[1] Marlene Targ Brill, *John Adams: Second President of the United States* (Chicago: Children's Press, 1986), 66.

© COPYRIGHT, The Center for Learning. Used with permission. Not for resale.

Name _____

Date _____

Biography Views

Values & Goals

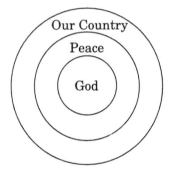

Nicknames

Had these: *Should have had these:*

His Rotundity   Old #2
                                 Just Missed

John Adams

- We're both short.
- We both like to write.
- Neither of us likes to travel.

Similarities

Compared to ME

Differences

- He often stood up to the crowd.
- He didn't have many friends.
- He held grudges a long time.

How I Rate This Person

(1–10, 10=Best)

Human Warmth | 4 |

Courage | 9 |

Successes | 8 |

Comments: Mr. Adams had many frustrations.

© COPYRIGHT, The Center for Learning. Used with permission. Not for resale.

Social Studies Activities
U.S. History and Geography 1
Lesson 8
Handout 22 (page 1)

Name _____

Date _____

A Brief Biography

```
┌─────────────────────────────────────────────────────┐
│                                                       │
│                                                       │
└─────────────────────────────────────────────────────┘
```

_____

_____

_____

_____

_____

_____

_____

_____

_____

_____

_____

_____

_____

_____

_____

_____

_____

_____

_____

_____

_____

_____

© COPYRIGHT, The Center for Learning. Used with permission. Not for resale.

Name _____

Date _____

Biography Timeline

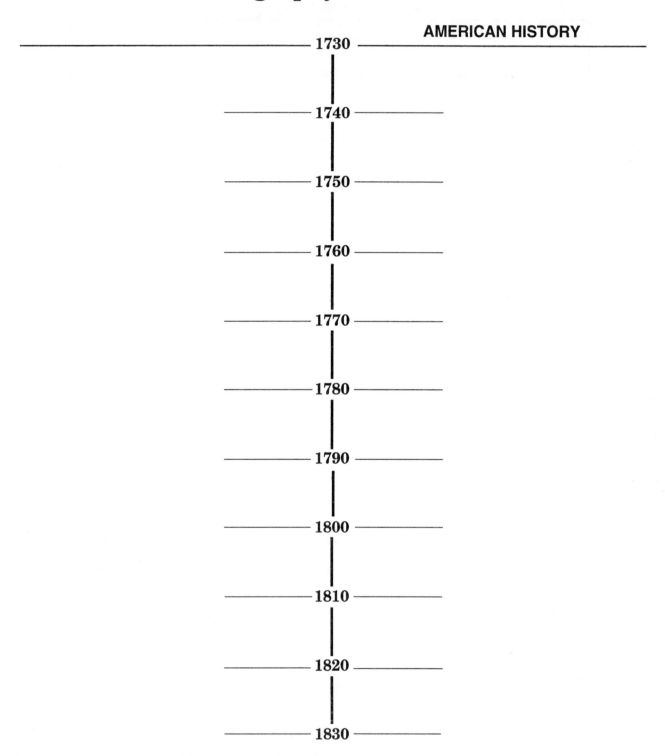

AMERICAN HISTORY

1730

1740

1750

1760

1770

1780

1790

1800

1810

1820

1830

© COPYRIGHT, The Center for Learning. Used with permission. Not for resale.

Social Studies Activities
U.S. History and Geography 1
Lesson 8
Handout 22 (page 3)

Name _____

Date _____

Biography Views

Key Quotes:

_____

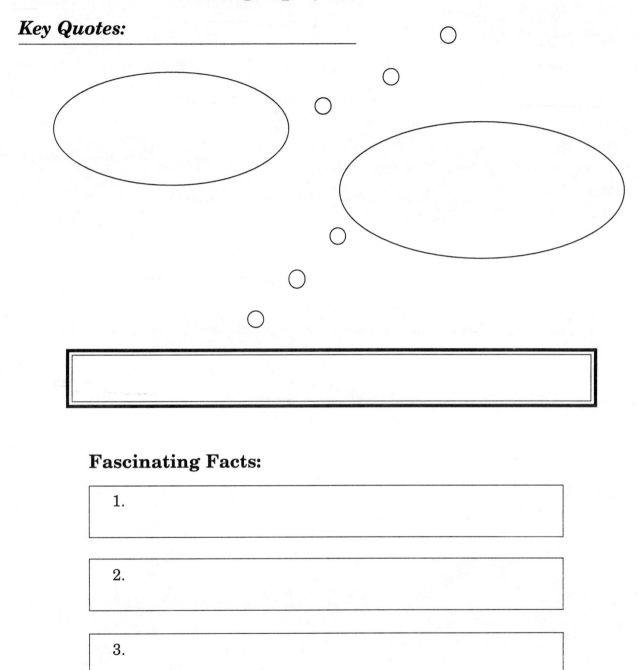

Fascinating Facts:

1.

2.

3.

© COPYRIGHT, The Center for Learning. Used with permission. Not for resale.

Name _____

Date _____

Biography Views

Values & Goals

Nicknames

Had these: *Should have had these:*

_____   _____

_____   _____

_____

_____

_____

Similarities

Compared to ME

Differences

_____

_____

_____

How I Rate This Person

(1-10, 10=Best)

Human Warmth ☐

Courage ☐

Successes ☐

Comments: _____

_____

© COPYRIGHT, The Center for Learning. Used with permission. Not for resale.

Lesson 9

Stamps

Objectives

- To increase interest in U.S. history through exploration of U.S. Postage stamps
- To learn about Benjamin Bannekar
- To understand the significance of the Erie Canal

Interdisciplinary Strands

Language Arts, Art

Notes to the Teacher

There is more behind stamps than just glue. There are stories of high adventure and matchless courage, of war and hardship and political high drama.[1]
—*Gordon Morison, Assistant Postmaster General*

There are over nineteen million stamp collectors in the United States today. Most of them were introduced to philately before they were sixteen years old. For these individuals, a vital link between history, geography, and their hobby exists—lifelong learning at its best.

To complete this lesson, students need a variety of U.S. postage stamps or pictures thereof. The sources listed below, especially the current edition of *The Postal Service Guide to U.S. Stamps* are useful.

Prior to teaching the lesson, collect stamps. Students can save stamps over a period of several weeks. Local businesses are often willing to provide canceled stamps. The school office is an excellent stamp source.

The description of the stamp selection process in Enrichment/Extension is an accurate one and is open to students. Actually, submitting a design is not necessary, just the idea and appropriate background information.

The U.S. Postal Service sponsor school stamp clubs. They currently have over 900,000 members. Their services include separate newsletters for teachers and students, stamp activity guides, and film loans. To participate, contact:

U.S. Postal Service Ben Franklin Stamp Club Program
Washington, D.C. 20260-7655

MATERIALS:
Handouts 23 and 24, U.S. postage stamps or books with pictures of stamps, reference materials

[1] U.S. Postal Service, *The Postal Service Guide to U.S. Stamps* (Washington, D.C., U.S. Postal Service, 1988), 6.

77

TERMS:
astronomer, canal, commemorative, philately, surveyor

Resources

1. Andrest, Ralph K. *The Erie Canal.* New York: American Heritage Publishing Co., Inc., 1964.

2. Bloomgarden, Henry S. *American History through Commemorative Stamps.* New York: Arco Publishing Company, Inc., 1969.

3. Lewis, Clause. *Benjamin Bannekar: The Man Who Saved Washington.* New York: McGraw-Hill Inc., 1970.

4. Tower, Samuel A. *A Stamp Collector's History of the United States.* New York: The New York Times, 1975.

5. U.S. Postal Service, *The Postal Service Guide to U.S. Stamps.* Washington, D.C.: U.S. Postal Service, 1988.

A teaching unit which begins with colonial America, outlines the settlement of territories, and covers the formation of the states is available for $2.00 from American Stamp Dealers Association, 3 School Street, Glen Cove, NY 11042.

Procedure

1. Ask students if they know anyone who collects stamps. Chances are that they are collectors or know someone who is. Emphasize the hobby aspect of philately. Discuss the use of postage stamps to commemorate important people and events. Show some commemorative stamps or pictures of them.

2. Use **Handout 23** to discuss Benjamin Bannekar as an American historical figure. Locate Maryland; Annapolis, Md.; the District of Columbia; and Washington, D.C. on a wall map. Note that this stamp is part of the Black Heritage Series and point out that groups, as well as individuals, are honored.

3. Have students select five categories (*e.g.*, inventors, women, American presidents) worthy of commemoration by a stamp series and list at least three persons in each category who deserve to be so honored (Thomas Edison, Rachel Carson, Woodrow Wilson).

4. Use **Handout 23**, page 2 to discuss the significance of the opening of the Erie Canal. Trace its route on a wall map. Emphasize its economic impact on the young nation. Have students select five categories of events in American history (*e.g.*, medical discoveries, social/cultural events, battles) worthy of recognition in a stamp series and list at least five items in each category (discovery of the Salk polio vaccine, erection of America's first skyscraper, Perry's victory on Lake Erie).

5. Remind students that stamps tell stories about our country and its people. Have students design two commemorative stamps—one person and one event. They must select the person and event, research each, draw the stamps, and record the information on **Handout 24**.

6. Use the persons, events and student-drawn stamps for oral reports and classroom bulletin board displays.

Enrichment/Extension

1. Replicate the activity by having students select a country and research a person or event depicted in its postage stamps.

2. Invite a stamp collector or dealer to visit class and talk about philately.

3. Bring in some stamps from other countries and have students compare and contrast the foreign and American stamps.

4. Most stamp ideas come from citizens. Six times a year, a committee of artists, historians, business people, and stamp collectors meets to review proposals which have been submitted suggesting new stamps which should be issued. If the committee accepts an idea, a professional artist is hired to design the stamp. This process takes about three years.

5. Have students, individually or in groups, think of an individual or event they consider worthy of commemoration on a stamp. Have them describe the stamp—they can also draw the stamp—and write a short essay explaining why the U.S. Postal Service should issue it. Help students send their recommendations to the committee at the following address:

   United States Postal Service Citizens' Stamp Advisory Committee
   Room 5670
   475 L'Enfant Plaza West, SW
   Washington, D.C. 20260-6753

Name _____

Date _____

A Stamp Star

Who: Benjamin Bannekar

When Issued: February 15, 1980

Where Issued: Annapolis, Maryland

Why Honored: First Black presidential
appointment—1791 by George Washington

Brief Biography: He was born free in 1731 near Baltimore,
Maryland. He was the grandson of an African chief who had been
brought to America as a slave. His grandmother taught him to
read. He was an astronomer, essayist, mathematician, inventor,
almanac publisher, and surveyor. He became a city planner when
he was appointed to help establish the boundaries of the District of
Columbia and lay out the new nation's capital city of Washington,
D.C. He died on his farm in 1806.

Source: Adapted from *Postmasters of America Philatelic First Day Covers* (Washington, D.C.: National Association of
Postmasters and National League of Postmasters, 1980), Not Paged.

© COPYRIGHT, The Center for Learning. Used with permission. Not for resale.

Name _____

Date _____

A Memorable Event in Stamps

What: The Opening of the Erie Canal

When Issued: October 26, 1980

Where Issued: Buffalo, New York

Why Issued: To commemorate the 155th anniversary of the opening of the Erie Canal

Brief Description of the Event: On October 26, 1825, when New York Governor DeWitt Clinton opened the 363-mile, seven million dollar Erie Canal, it was the culmination of a dream. Inland Americans had long wanted an easy route to the East Coast that would not mean crossing the Appalachian Mountains. The Erie Canal was begun in 1817. It was a great engineering feat. It was dug by hand and grew slowly at the rate of one mile a week. The Erie Canal opened the West to settlement. It was an economic success because it (1) made it possible to ship raw materials to manufacturing plants in the East and Europe from inland America by a water route, and (2) provided a way to ship finished products to the frontier by water routes.

Source: Adapted from *The American Heritage Collection of Epic Events in American History* (Cheyenne, Wyo.: Fleetwood, 1979), Not Paged.

© COPYRIGHT, The Center for Learning. Used with permission. Not for resale.

Name _____

Date _____

My Stamp Star

Who: _____

When Issued: _____

Where Issued: _____

Why Honored: _____

Brief Biography: _____

_____

_____

_____

_____

_____

_____

_____

_____

_____

Source: _____

_____

© COPYRIGHT, The Center for Learning. Used with permission. Not for resale.

Name _____

Date _____

My Memorable Stamp Event

What: _____

When Issued: _____

Where Issued: _____

Why Issued: _____

Brief Description of the Event: _____

_____

_____

_____

_____

_____

_____

_____

_____

_____

_____

_____

Source: _____

_____

© COPYRIGHT, The Center for Learning. Used with permission. Not for resale.

Native American Acrostics

Objectives

- To do research on famous Native Americans
- To learn how to make an acrostic
- To learn about Tecumseh

Interdisciplinary Strands

English/Language Arts, Art

Notes to the Teacher

The "fad" to teach about minorities and the fact that it was "in" to study "the plight of the American Indian" has not resulted in the hoped for increased understanding of Native American cultures and contributions. This lesson is designed to use a research activity to help students learn more about famous Native American leaders.

Although Tecumseh is featured on the sample activity sheet, encourage students to select persons across the entire range of United States history. Some research selections are Pochantas, John Ross, Osceola, Crazy Horse, Blue Jacket, Geronimo, Sequoya, Black Hawk, Massasoit, Maria Tallchief, Sitting Bull, Chief Joseph, Chochise, Squanto, Sacajewea, Pontiac, Little Crow, Logan, Hiawatha, Ira Hayes, and Vine Deloria, Jr.

The acrostic is a technique easily adapted to a broad range of topics and content. It is as valuable, perhaps more valuable, for students to make acrostics than it is for them to solve them. Once they have mastered how to construct acrostics, students enjoy doing them. They are popular homework assignments.

MATERIALS:
Handouts 25 and **26**, reference books, trade books, biographies, collective biographies

TERMS:
acrostic, confederacy, destined, league, legend, recruiting, trickle

Resources

1. Andrest, Ralph K. *The Long Death*. New York: The Macmillan Company, 1964.

2. Freedman, Russell. *Indian Chiefs*. New York: Holiday House, 1987.

3. Heuman, William. *Famous American Indians*. New York: Dodd, Mead and Company, 1972.

4. Joseph, Alvin M., Jr. *The Patriot Chiefs*. New York: The Viking Press, 1961.

5. LaFarge, Oliver. *The American Indian.* New York: Golden Press, Inc., 1960.

6. Maxwell, James A., ed. *America's Fascinating Indian Heritage.* Pleasantville, N.Y.: The Readers Digest Association, Inc., 1978.

7. Terrell, John Upton. *Apache Chronicle.* New York: World Publishing, 1972.

8. Vogel, Virgil J. *This Country Was Ours: A Documentary History of the American Indian.* New York: Harper and Row Publishers, 1977.

Biographies and collective biographies of famous Native Americans

Procedure

1. Ask students to name some Native Americans, and list their names on the chalkboard. After a list has been compiled, ask students to give three important facts about each of one of the persons listed. Do not let them cheat—he was a man or she was a women; he or she is dead! It should become apparent that we know many names but possess scant information about Native Americans.

2. Help students speculate why this is so. The impact of Hollywood and television on our knowledge of this ethnic group will feature prominently in the tracing of our perceptions and the depth of our understanding.

3. Explain that each student is to select a Native American, read about him or her, and write a short biographical sketch of the subject. If Tecumseh was not listed earlier, introduce him and distribute **Handout 25**. Read the biography and locate on a wall map the places significant in Tecemseh's life.

4. Have students solve the acrostic on page 3 of **Handout 25**. Tell them that the answers can be found in the biography they have just read. Review correct responses with them.
   Suggested Responses, Handout 25:

1.	*Battle*	4.	*Thames*
2.	*Ohio*	5.	*confederacy*
3.	*Canada*	6.	*Shawnee*

5. Using the directions at the end of the biography and the acrostic, review how to construct an acrostic. Note the arrowhead used as a symbol for the background. Draw from students possible symbols they can use in their acrostics. Use a wall map to locate various tribal areas and suggest possibilities— Eastern Woodland Indians, a long house; Plains Indians, an Indian pony; Southwest Indians, a hogan; Indians of the Northwest, a totem. Use the Notes to the Teacher to help them decide on a person to research. Encourage them to use the index of their textbooks for additional ideas.

6. Assign **Handout 26**, page 1.

7. When students have completed the biography assignment, distribute **Handout 26**, page 2. Review, again, how to construct an acrostic, and have students draw the symbol they have selected and construct an acrostic. Remind them to put the answers upside down on the bottom of the page. The acrostic itself is not to be filled in.

8. Have students exchange acrostics and try to solve each other's puzzles.

Enrichment/Extension

1. Select one or two and have them put on transparencies for the entire class to solve.

2. Display the acrostics and have a contest to see which student(s) can solve the most correctly.

3. Replicate the activity using other content from American or world history.

Social Studies Activities
U.S. History and Geography 1
Lesson 10
Handout 25 (page 1)—*Sample*

Name _____

Date _____

Tecumseh: The Story of a Native American

Around 1768 in a Shawnee town near the site of modern-day Piqua, Ohio, a baby boy was born who was destined to become a famous chief. Legends claim that he showed signs of great leadership skills at a young age.

Settlers were moving across the Appalachian Mountains into the Ohio country. Tecumseh did not like what was happening to his people, to all native Americans in fact. When he became a chief, he looked for ways to push the settlers back to the Atlantic Ocean.

One idea he had was to side with the British against the Americans in the Revolutionary War. He thought that the British would not want to settle on tribal land. He knew that the trickle of American settlers was fast becoming a flood.

Another plan to keep tribal land was Tecumseh's Indian League. He wanted all the tribes to forget their differences and unite against the settlers. He traveled far and wide urging tribes to form a confederacy which could resist those who were taking their land.

Unfortunately, Tecumseh was away on one of his recruiting trips and his brother, Elskwatawa, a medicine man known as "the Prophet," was in charge when soldiers attacked a Shawnee camp on the Tippecanoe River. The Prophet fought William Henry Harrison's troops and lost the Battle of Tippecanoe.

Tecumseh continued to resist the Americans, but things did not go well for native Americans. In the War of 1812, Tecumseh again fought on the side of the British. He was killed in the Battle of the Thames in 1813. Thus, his unknown grave is in Canada north of Detroit, Michigan. In life, Tecumseh could not save the Ohio country for his people. In death, he did not manage to save even enough for his own grave and lies buried in another country.[1]

---

[1] Russell Shorto, *Tecumseh and the Dream of an American Indian Nation* (Englewood Cliffs, N.J.: SIlver Burdett Press, 1989).

© COPYRIGHT, The Center for Learning. Used with permission. Not for resale.

Social Studies Activities
U.S. History and Geography 1
Lesson 10
Handout 25 (page 2)

Name _____

Date _____

How to Make an Acrostic

1. Select a significant symbol for the person who is the subject of your acrostic. Draw the symbol as background for the puzzle part (top) of the acrostic.

2. Select a significant key word for the person who is the subject of your acrostic. Write that word, letter at a time and line at a time, vertically down the center of the top of the acrostic. The word should be no less than five letters and no more than eight letters long. In the left hand margin, number the line for each letter.

3. Use each letter in the key word as part of another word that has significance in the life of the acrostic person. Place blanks for the letters other than the letter which appears in the key word. Note that the key word letter can appear any place in the clue word. Jot down the word, in order, that you have selected for your acrostic on a separate piece of paper. Be sure to count the blanks you have drawn and compare them with your list. It will be impossible to solve your acrostic if the blanks are not correctly placed.

4. Using your list of selected words, write clues that help identify the horizontal words that fit into the blanks. Construct your clues carefully so that the person solving your acrostic will be able to identify the *one* word that you want as an answer.

5. Upside down at the bottom of the page, write the answers.

© COPYRIGHT, The Center for Learning. Used with permission. Not for resale.

Name _____

Date _____

An Acrostic of a Native American

1.   _ _ _ T _ _ _

2.   _ H _ _

3.   _ _ _ A _ _

4.   _ _ _ M _ _

5.   _ _ _ _ _ E _ _ _ _ _

6.   S _ _ _ _ _ _

Clues:

1. Indians lost the_____of Tippecanoe to William Henry Harrison.

2. Tecumseh was born in what is now the state of_____.

3. Tecumseh is buried north of Detroit in the country of_____.

4. Tecumseh was killed in the Battle of the_____.

5. Tecumseh tried to form a_____of Indian tribes.

6. Tecumseh was a member of the_____tribe.

Answers: 1. *Battle*, 2. *Ohio*, 3. *Canada*, 4. *Thames*, 5. *confederacy*, 6. *Shawnee*

© COPYRIGHT, The Center for Learning. Used with permission. Not for resale.

Name _____

Date _____

_____ My Story of a Native American

_____

_____

_____

_____

_____

_____

_____

_____

_____

_____

_____

_____

_____

_____

_____

_____

_____

_____

_____

_____

_____

_____

Source: _____

_____

   © COPYRIGHT, The Center for Learning. Used with permission. Not for resale.

Social Studies Activities
U.S. History and Geography 1
Lesson 10
Handout 26 (page 2)

Name _____

Date _____

My Acrostic of a Native American

_____

_____

_____

_____

_____

_____

_____

_____

_____

_____

_____

Clues: _____

_____

_____

_____

_____

_____

_____

_____

_____

_____

_____

© COPYRIGHT, The Center for Learning. Used with permission. Not for resale.

Music of Slavery

Objectives

- To investigate slave songs of antebellum America
- To explore music as social history in time and place
- To study the spiritual, "Go Down, Moses"

Interdisciplinary Strands

English/Language Arts, Music

Notes to the Teacher

This lesson is designed to follow the study of slave life in pre-Civil War America. It should help dispel the old Hollywood stereotype of the happy, contented slaves singing in their quarters.

Songbooks and actual recordings may be available from the school's music department or the local public library. Use them if they can be obtained.

Some possible spirituals students may research are *Steal Away; Now Let Me Fly; Nobody Knows De Trouble I See; One More River; Sit Down, Sister; My Lord What a Morning; Jacob's Ladder; Roll, Jordan, Roll; Follow the Drinking Gourd;* and *Swing Low, Sweet Chariot.*

Asking students to decipher the possible double meanings of slavery's songs is assigning a difficult task. The religious overtones and symbols, which were crystal clear to the slaves and others of that time, are unclear and confusing to today's children. Permit them to work together; they can help one another. Stand ready to offer assistance.

MATERIALS:
Handouts 27 and **28**, reference books, songbooks

TERMS:
ineffable, pharaoh, spirituals, woe

Resources

1. Boni, Margaret Bradford, selector. *Favorite American Songs.* New York: Simon & Schuster, Inc., 1956.

   _____: *Fireside Book of Folk Songs.* New York: Simon & Schuster, Inc., 1967. 17th Printing.

Procedure

1. Ask students to name some "happy" songs and some "sad" songs. List these on the chalkboard under appropriate headings. Ask students if they think

songs sung by the slaves were happy songs or sad songs and why. Answers will vary.

2. Introduce Frederick Douglass by asking students if they know who he was. If he is unknown to them and sufficient information is not in their textbooks, briefly tell his story. Locate Maryland on a wall map.

3. Allow time for students to read page 1 of **Handout 27** silently. Read it aloud and discuss Frederick Douglas's view of slave music as the selection is being read. Emphasize that spirituals may not be as they first appear.

4. Review the lyrics of page 2, **Handout 27** and be certain the students understand their religious connotations. Read and discuss the possible interpretation and double meaning of the lyrics. Play the spiritual if a recording is available.

5. Make reference materials and songbooks available to students in the classroom, or take them to the library. Have each student select a spiritual and complete **Handout 28**'s writing assignment.

6. Have students share their songs and explain the lyrics—both literally and figuratively. If possible, have the class sing some of the spirituals.

7. Display the completed handouts and make them part of the *My American History Book* if the activity is a class project.

Enrichment/Extension

1. After analyzing "Go Down, Moses" place the following quote on the chalkboard:
   > "The themes of death, release, and escape which run through the spiritual have a double meaning: first, a literal and practical longing for a better life after death; second, a symbolic identification with the Israelites who, in their passage from Egypt, symbolize the escape of the Black races from White domination."[1]

   Have students compare their responses on **Handout 27**, page 2 with what an "expert" thinks.

2. Have students, individually or in small groups, sing—or present in choral reading style—spirituals they researched for work on **Handout 28**.

3. Have students research and report on folk songs of other time periods of American history or other sectors of American society. Labor union songs and political campaign songs are easy to find.

4. Encourage students to research and report on folk songs from other lands. Most libraries have folk song songbooks, featuring other countries.

[1] Denis Arnold, gen. ed., *The New Oxford Companion to Music, Volume 2* (New York: OxfordUniversity Press, 1983), 1739–1740.

Social Studies Activities
U.S. History and Geography 1
Lesson 11
Handout 27 (page 1)—*Sample*

Name _____

Date _____

An Ex-Slave's View of their Music

Frederick Douglass was born a slave in 1818 in Maryland. He escaped in 1838. Seven years later, in 1845, he published a book in which he described what it was like to be a slave. This is what he had to say about the songs sung by slaves.

"Slaves were expected to sing as well as to work. Neither masters nor overseers liked a silent slave, and the cries 'Make a noise there! Make a noise there! Bear a hand!' were heard when slaves became silent. The fact that they were expected to sing . . . may be the reason for the almost constant singing among the slaves when they were at their work. Those who drove teams of animals sang at all times. Thus, even if the overseer was far away from them, he knew where the slaves were and what they were doing."

". . . people often said that slaves were the most contented and happy laborers in the world. Their dancing and singing were thought to be proof of this fact. But it was a great mistake to suppose slaves were happy because they sometimes made those joyful noises. The slave songs expressed their sorrows rather than their joys. Like tears, they were a relief to aching hearts. The human mind often uses the same method for expressing opposite emotions. Slave songs were full of sorrow and bleakness as well as joy and peace."[1]

---

[1] Frederick Douglass, *From Slave to Statesman: The Life and Times of Frederick Douglass,* abridged by Glenn Munson (New York: Noble and Noble, Publishers, Inc., 1972), 34–35.

© COPYRIGHT, The Center for Learning. Used with permission. Not for resale.

Name _____

Date _____

A Slave Songbook
"Go Down Moses"[1]

When Israel was in Egypt land,
Let my people go.
Oppressed so hard, she could not stand,
Let my people go.
Go down, Moses, Way down in Egypt land,
Tell old Pharaoh to let my people go.

Thus spoke the Lord, bold Moses said,
Let my people go,
"If not, I'll strike your firstborn dead,"
Let my people go.
Go down, Moses, Way down in Egypt land,
Tell old Pharaoh to let my people go.

This song is based on the Bible story of how Moses led the Hebrew people out of bondage in the land of Egypt. It has many verses.

Some people think it expressed the slave's hope that they too would be led out of bondage. Pharaoh would be the slave owner or master. Moses would be the person who would lead the slaves to freedom. Harriet Tubman was known as the "Moses of Her People" because she led so many slaves north to freedom on the Underground Railroad.

[1] Margaret Bradford Boni, selector, *Fireside Book of Folk Songs* (New York: Simon and Schuster, Inc., 1967), 324–325.

© COPYRIGHT, The Center for Learning. Used with permission. Not for resale.

Name _____

Date _____

My Slave Songbook

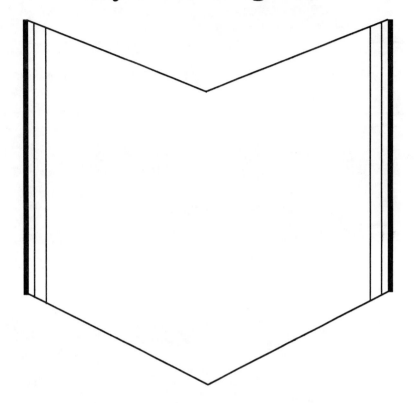

_____

_____

_____

_____

_____

_____

_____

_____

Source: _____

_____

_____

© COPYRIGHT, The Center for Learning. Used with permission. Not for resale.

Name Origins

Objectives

- To develop awareness of ethnic origins
- To explore the origins of surnames
- To learn about the origins of Martin Van Buren's names

Interdisciplinary Strands

English/Language Arts, Art

Notes to the Teacher

This lesson uses students' fascination with names to inquire into the ethnic background of famous Americans and of local families. It dovetails easily with a study of immigration to the United States. It is an introduction to the study of genealogy.

There are about 1,250,000 surnames in the United States. As people who research their family trees discover there is a story in every one of them. Acquire some of the recommended resources on names, so students will be able to learn the story of their own names (and/or other surnames in their families) and see where some of their friends' families are from.

Last names were used by some groups in antiquity but then the practice died out in Europe, to be revived in the tenth century. According to Lambert and Pei[1] surnames the world over tend to derive from four common types of descriptors:

1.	The father's name	Peterson, Johnson
2.	The place where the family lived	Atwell, Hillman
3.	The person's trade or profession	Carpenter, Smith
4.	A description of the person	Goodman, Armstrong

Share some caveats with students early because name research is a tricky business. Many names have been deliberately (to avoid discrimination) or accidentally (errors in spelling) changed. For example, countless individuals received new surnames at Ellis Island. "Oh, that's too hard to pronounce. We'll make your last name 'Fish.'" Handouts contains helpful hints for linking last names with their national origins. Students will have to be reminded, however, that these rules are not ironclad. While it is true that many German names end in-**man**, it is not, therefore, true that all names ending in-**man** are German. Similarly, though many names ending in -**ov** are Russian, not all Russian names end in -**ov**. For these reasons availability of reference books on names is important for the success of this lesson.

---

[1] Lambert, Eloise and Mario Pei, *Our Names: Where They Came from and What They Mean.* (New York: Lothrop, Lee & Shepard Co., 1960), 71–98.

Students need to know that surname tracing is based on language differences so what one learns is not always the country of origin. For example, identifying a name like Gomez as Spanish doesn't tell us whether the family came from Mexico, Peru, Spain, or any number of Spanish-speaking countries. Ultimately, this family's roots probably do trace back to Spain, however.

Students need time and encouragement to find out about their own names (first, last, and middle) and surnames common in their community. This exercise can form a vital link between students' worlds and the ones they're reading about in their textbooks.

MATERIALS:
Handouts 29, 30, 31 and 32, reference books on names, crayons, scissors, clothesline, string

TERMS:
genealogy, origin, surname

Resources

1. Clarke, Joseph H. *Pseudonyms: The Names Behind the Names.* Nashville: Thomas Nelson, Inc., 1977.

2. Hazen, Barbara Shook. *Last, First, Middle and Nick: All About Names* Englewood Cliffs, N.J.: Prentice-Hall, Inc., 1979.

3. Hook, J. N. *Family Names: How Our Surnames Came to America.* New York: Macmillan Publishing Co., Inc., 1982.

4. Lambert, Eloise, and Mario Pei. *Our Names: Where They Came from and What They Mean.* New York: Lothrop, Lee & Shepard Co., 1960.

5. Lee, Mary Price. *Your Name—All About It.* Philadelphia: The Westminster Press, 1980.

6. Lee, Mary Price, and Richard S Lee. *Last Names First.* Philadelphia: Westminster Press, 1985.

7. Meltzer, Milton. *A Book About Names.* New York: Thomas Y. Crowell, 1984.

8. Seletsky, Alice. "My Name Is Alice: A Fifth Grade Story of Naming and Family History," in Vincent Rogers, et al., eds., *Teaching Social Studies: Portraits from the Classroom,* Bulletin No. 82. Washington, D.C.: National Council for the Social Studies, 1988, 10–18.

9. Smith, Elsdon C. *New Dictionary of American Family Names.* New York: Harper & Row Publishers, 1973.

Procedure

1. Ask students if they know what the origins of their last names are. Ask if they know any ways to recognize what country a name came from. Answers will vary. Tell students that there are over 1,250,000 last names in the United States: one can identify the origins of many of these names by the use of some general guidelines based on language clues. Inform them that they are going to study name origins. Use the Notes to the Teacher to provide some background information.

2. Ask students who Martin Van Buren was. Ask if they can guess the origins of any of his names. Ask if they know any of his nicknames. Answers will vary, but most should know him as a U.S. President and some may know at least one of his nicknames.

3. Use **Handout 29** to discuss the origins of Martin Van Buren's names. On a world map or globe, locate Kinderhook, N.Y., Holland, and Germany.

4. Review the name origins chart in **Handout 30.** Locate the countries on a wall map and have students note the continents on which they can be found. Explain that these name origins are only guidelines and that they should be used in conjunction with other sources, especially reference books on names. Note that Martin Van Buren's surname fits the guidelines.

5. Familiarize students with available reference books on name origins. Point out that these books usually tell the original meaning of a name as well as its national origin.

6. Have students select a famous American and research the origins of his/her names. Encourage students to select from a broad range of categories, sports figures, writers, scientists, political figures—and encourage them to select women and minorities. Consider assigning the research as homework. Record research results on **Handout 31**.

7. When students have completed the handout, have them share the results of their research. Total the number of names of each national origin. Record the totals on the chalkboard. Use a wall map and/or globe to locate the countries and continents of the persons researched.

8. Remind students that all surnames—obscure as well as famous ones—can be traced to a nation of origin in most cases. Tell students that they are going to do research on six surnames in their community. Their family surname counts as one of the six.

9. Each student will need two copies of **Handout 32**. Have students select six community surnames and write the names in the slots on the buildings. Instruct students to write the results of their research on the back of the building and to *underline* the national origin of the name. Have students cut out and color the buildings using the following color code:

> Africa: shades of green
> Asia: shades of blue
> Australia: shades of yellow
> Europe: shades of red
> North America: shades of brown
> South America: shades of orange

Be certain that the students use varying shades. It is a good reminder for them that people are not of uniform color—only generally the same color. All Africans are not black; all Asians are not yellow; and all Europeans are not white.

10. Share the results of the Surname City research. Have students cut out their completed buildings. Hang a clothesline and attach the buildings along the line. Place the clothesline so that both sides of the buildings can be seen. Note: The buildings can be hung from the ceiling on strings of various lengths for display purposes if a clothesline is impractical.

Enrichment/Extension

1. Have students use **Handout 31** and research famous persons of foreign countries.

2. Discuss why people change their names. Have a group of students research the legal process for a name change and report to the class.

3. Have students research the "real" names or nicknames of entertainers. Who did Archibald Leach become? What is Vanna White's "real" name? How did Marion Michael Morrison (John Wayne) get the nickname "Duke?" (Answers: Cary Grant; Vanna Marie Rosick; as a youngster he had a pet airedale terrier whose name was Duke and they were so inseparable that people gave them one name—the dog's!)

Name _____

Date _____

A President's Names

First: Martin

Comes from the Latin meaning of Mars; warlike.[1]

_____

_____

_____

_____

Middle: None Given

_____

_____

_____

_____

Last: Van Büren

Van—Dutch preposition meaning of or from; used with Dutch family names, originally designating where the family came from or received its name.[2] Büren is a city in western Germany.[3] This may be the ancestral home of this family.

[1] *Funk and Wagnells Standard Dictionary of the English Language*, International Edition, I (Chicago, Encyclopedia Britannica, Inc., 1965), 783.

[2] Ibid., II, 1387.

[3] John Dodge, ex. ed., *Encyclopedia Britannica World Atlas* (Chicago: Encyclopedia Britannica, Inc., William Benton, Publisher, 1964), 17.

© COPYRIGHT, The Center for Learning. Used with permission. Not for resale.

Social Studies Activities
U.S. History and Geography 1
Lesson 12
Handout 29 (page 2)—*Sample*

Name _____

Date _____

Nickname(s)

Nickname(s)

1. "The Little Magician"—because of his political ability.[4]

2. "The Red Fox of Kinderhook"—because he had red sideburns and John Calhoun compared him to a fox.[5]

3. "The American Talleyrand"—because he was a shrewd political manager like Talleyrand, the European diplomat.[6]

4. "Little Van"—because he was only 5'6" tall.[7]

5. "Old Kinderhook"—because he retired to his hometown of Kinderhook, N.Y.[8]

---

[4] Louis W. Loenig, "The Rise of the Little Magician," *American Heritage*, XIII, No. 4, June 1962, 31.

[5] Ibid.

[6] John A. Garraty, *1,001 Things Everyone Should Know About American History* (New York: Doubleday, 1989), 8.

[7] Robert C. Post, ed., *Every Four Years* (Washington, D.C.: Smithsonian Books, 1984), 60.

[8] Ibid., 71.

© COPYRIGHT, The Center for Learning. Used with permission. Not for resale.

Name _____

Date _____

Where Names Came From

Language	Special Features of Names	Examples
African	Most freed slaves adopted common American names after the Civil War.	Washington, Williams, Smith, Harris, Green
Arabic	Begin with ibn Two syllable names that begin with H-	Ibn Hassan, Ibn Ibrahim Haddad, Hassan, Hakim, Harrar
Chinese	Short surnames	Wong, Lee, Ho, Chang, Chiang, Lan, Li, Chan
Dutch	Begin with Van- Begin with Ten	Vandike, Van Raalte Ten Eyck, Ten Broek
English	Describe old occupations Made of simple English words	Smith, Hunter, Baker, Carpenter, Cook, White, Churchill, Brown, Underwood
French	Begin with Du- Begin with Le- End in -er	Dubois, Dupont, Dupré Leclerc, Lejeune Meunier, Lanier, Jacquier
German	Containing vowels with ¨ Ends with-man or -mann End with -berg or -burg	Müller, Grün, Schäfer Zimmermann, Gutman Weinberg, Muhlenburg
Hebrew	Begin with Levi- Use old Hebrew names	Levi, Levin, Levine, Levinson Cohen, Ephraim, Hyman
Irish	Begin with O'- Begin with Mc- Begin with Fitz	O'Hara, O'Brien, O'Neil McCarthy, McGuire Fitzgerald, Fitzhugh
Italian	Use di or de	de Stefano, De Rosa DiMarco, DiMaggio
Japanese	Begin with Yama- End with -mura or-moto	Yamoto, Yamada Nakamura, Matsumoto

© COPYRIGHT, The Center for Learning. Used with permission. Not for resale.

Social Studies Activities
U.S. History and Geography 1
Lesson 12
Handout 30 (page 2)—*Sample*

Name _____

Date _____

Language	Special Features of Names	Examples
Korean	Short surnames	Yu, Ko, Kim, Shin, Park
Native Americans	Based on things found in nature	Black Hawk, Deernose, Thunder Cloud
Polish	End in -ski	Kowalski, Sucharski
Russian	End in -ov	Ivanov, Petrov, Popov
Scandinavian	End in -son or -sen End in -dahl	Hansen, Larson, Olson Holmdahl, Linddahl
Scottish	Begin with -Mac-	Macdonald, Macleod
Spanish	End in -o End in -ez Begin with de, del, de los, de las	Bianco, Moreno, Santiago Perez, Lopez, Gomez del Rivero, De la Rosa
Vietnamese	Short surnames	Ba, Ky, Van, Chi, Minh

Source: Eloise Lambert and Mario Pei., *Our Names: Where They Came from and What They Mean* (New York: Lothrop, Lee & Shepard Co., 1960).

© COPYRIGHT, The Center for Learning. Used with permission. Not for resale.

Name _____

Date _____

The Name Game

First:

_____

_____

_____

_____

_____

Middle:

_____

_____

_____

_____

_____

Last:

_____

_____

_____

_____

_____

© COPYRIGHT, The Center for Learning. Used with permission. Not for resale.

Name _____

Date _____

Nickname:

_____

_____

_____

_____

_____

© COPYRIGHT, The Center for Learning. Used with permission. Not for resale.

Name _____

Date _____

Surname City

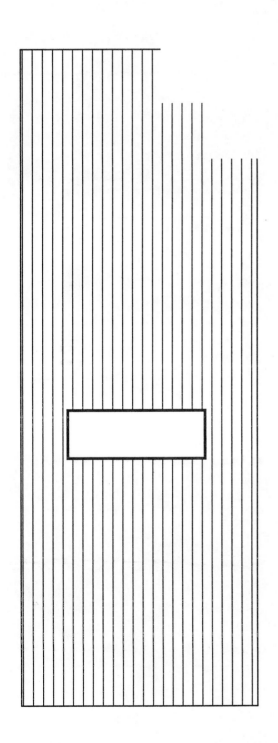

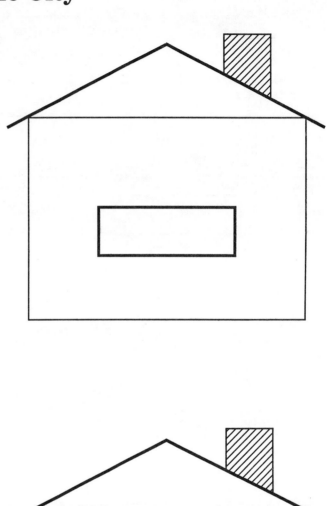

© COPYRIGHT, The Center for Learning. Used with permission. Not for resale.

McGuffey's Readers

Objectives

- To learn about William Holmes McGuffey
- To investigate *McGuffey's Readers* and their role in the teaching of morals
- To read and interpret poetry

Interdisciplinary Strands

English/Language Arts, Art, Career Education

Resources

1. *The Book of a Thousand Poems*. New York: Peter Bedrich Books, 1983.

2. Cole, William, ed. *The Poet's Tales*. New York: World Publishing, 1971.

3. Fisher, Leonard Everett. *The Schools*. New York: Holiday House, 1983.

4. Fujikawa, Guy, ed., *A Child's Book of Poems*. New York: Grosset and Dunlop, Inc., 1969.

5. *McGuffey's Eclectic Readers: Primer through the Sixth Grade*. New York: Van Nostrand Reinhold Company, Inc., N.D.

6. Minnich, Harvey C. *Old Favorites from the McGuffey Readers*. New York: American Book Company, 1936.

7. Revzin, Milton R. *McGuffey Reader Update, Homesite Edition*. Youngstown, Ohio: Scott Press, 1975.

8. Ross, David, ed. *The Illustrated Treasury of Poetry for Children*. New York: Grosset and Dunlop, Inc., 1970.

9. Westerhoff, Hohn H., III. *McGuffey and His Readers: Piety, Morality, and Education in Nineteenth-Century America*. Nashville, Tenn.: Abdington, 1978.

MATERIALS:
Handouts 33 and 34, gray construction paper, wood-grained contact paper, cardboard, felt tip pens, books of poetry

TERMS:
apt, reader, scholar, slate, the three Rs

Procedure

1. Write the following quote on the chalkboard:
   " 'Tis Education forms the common mind,
   Just as the twig is bent, the tree's inclin'd.' "[1]
   Alexander Pope

   Help students decode it. After they know what it means, ask if they agree or disagree and why. Answers will vary. Conduct a brief discussion which focuses on the impact of education . . . especially its impact on younger students in their formative years. Emphasize the factors which influence students especially teachers and textbooks.

2. Discuss teaching as a career choice. Introduce William Holmes McGuffey as both a teacher and a textbook author. Explain that his specialty was readers. Have students read the biography on **Handout 33**. Locate Ohio, Pennsylvania, Virginia, and Youngstown, Ohio on a U.S. wall map. If a modern reprint of a *McGuffey Reader* is available, read one or two selections to the class. Discuss the values (honesty, dignity of work, personal integrity, patriotism) that McGuffey taught.

3. Read the poem of **Handout 33** aloud, and help students interpret it. Emphasize the code of behavior (values) it teaches:

   - It is always better to tell the truth.
   - Speak the truth and you will be blessed.
   - Smile, it cheers up others.
   - Help others physically and emotionally.
   - Do not expect a reward for helping others.
   - Show your love for others by what you say and do.
   - Children, as well as adults, should do these things.

4. Have students browse through the collection of poetry books and select a short poem, or a verse from a longer poem, that contains a value they feel is worth remembering. Remind students of the hornbooks they learned about when they studied colonial America's schools. Introduce the school slate as its 19th century counterpart.

5. Distribute **Handout 34**. Have students cut it out, mount it on stiff cardboard, glue a sheet of light gray construction paper on the slate portion, cut strips of wood-grained contact paper, and glue them to the border to simulate the wooden frame. Monitor students as they write the poetry on their scholar's slate with felt tip pens.

6. Conduct a sharing session during which students show their slates, read the poetry selection, briefly explain its meaning, highlight the values it represents, and explain why they think those values should be part of our code of behavior or beliefs.

7. Make bulletin board display featuring the completed scholar slates.

Enrichment/Extension

1. Replicate the activity using paragraphs from famous American speeches, such as, Patrick Henry's "Liberty or Death Speech," Lincoln's "Gettysburg Address," FDR's "First Inaugural Address," Martin Luther King, Jr.'s "I Have a Dream Speech."

2. Use the scholar's slate exercise to illustrate American sayings. Some possible selections are:

   - Experience keeps a dear school but a fool will learn no other. (Benjamin Franklin)
   - Never put off until tomorrow what you can do today.
   - We are too soon old and too late smart. (Pennsylvania Dutch)[1]

---

[1] *The Oxford Dictionary of Quotations* (New York: Oxford University Press, 1980), 37.

Name _____

Date _____

The Man Behind
the McGuffey Readers

William Holmes McGuffey was born in Washington County, Pennsylvania on September 28, 1800. He was the firstborn child of Alexander McGuffey and Anna Holmes McGuffey. William did not remember Pennsylvania because the family moved West when he was only two years old.

His earliest memories were of Coitsville Township, near Youngstown, Ohio. His mother valued education and was happy that her eldest son was an eager and apt student. Eventually the family sent him away from home to be educated.

After McGuffey graduated from Pennsylvania training institutions, he became a teacher in Pennsylvania. He was only sixteen in 1816 when he was hired as a teacher. By 1826 Ohio had lured him back to be a college professor. By 1836, only ten years later, he was president of an Ohio college. Meanwhile, the McGuffey family became writers of readers.

Books were rare, and thus valued, on the frontier. As an educator, William Holmes McGuffey knew this. In 1836 he published his *First Reader;* it was 108 pages and cost twelve and one-half cents. Little did McGuffey know that this effort would continue through 555 editions (from 1836 to 1879) and sell over 122,000,000 copies! It is no wonder that he had to enlist the assistance of his family.

Harriet Spining McGuffey, his wife, wrote the first primer. It was published under his name; women were not readily accepted as authors at this time. When there was a demand for spellers to go with the readers, he had his brother, Alexander Hamilton McGuffey, assemble them.

© COPYRIGHT, The Center for Learning. Used with permission. Not for resale.

Social Studies Activities
U.S. History and Geography 1
Lesson 13
Handout 33 (page 2)—*Sample*

Name _____

Date _____

William Holmes McGuffey continued to be active as both a clergyman and educator while his books grew in popularity and use. Age sixty six found him traveling around the state of Virginia helping them establish public schools so that Virginia could be readmitted to the Union following the Civil War. He stayed active until his death in 1873.

The popularity of McGuffey's Readers continued after the death of William Holmes McGuffey. They were "American" in nature. The values they taught were American values. The lifestyle they featured was the American way of life. Generations of Americans were influenced by McGuffey.

In the last few years McGuffey's Readers have staged a comeback. They are available in a hardbound edition encased in a heavy cardboard container. More than 100 years after his death, yet another generation of Americans is getting a glimpse of the three Rs taught McGuffey style.[1]

[1] Milton R. Revzin, *McGuffey Reader Update, Homeside Edition* (Youngstown, Ohio: Scott Press, 1975).

© COPYRIGHT, The Center for Learning. Used with permission. Not for resale.

Social Studies Activities
U.S. History and Geography 1
Lesson 13
Handout 33 (page 3)—*Sample*

Name _____

Date _____

A 19th-Century Scholar's Slate

Truth and Love

'Tis a little thing to do
To speak the word that's true—
Yet truth is always best
And he who speaks it blest.

A smile's a little thing,
Yet never birds that sing
So sweetly grief beguile
As one who gives a smile.
other's pain,
Hoping for naught again,
Is what a child can do,
And find it easy, too.

And fairer than a star
Such deeds of kindness are—
Brighter than stars above
Are words of Truth and Love.[2]

Page 143 Second Reader

[2] Ibid., 39.

© COPYRIGHT, The Center for Learning. Used with permission. Not for resale.

Name _____

Date _____

My 20th-Century Scholar's Slate

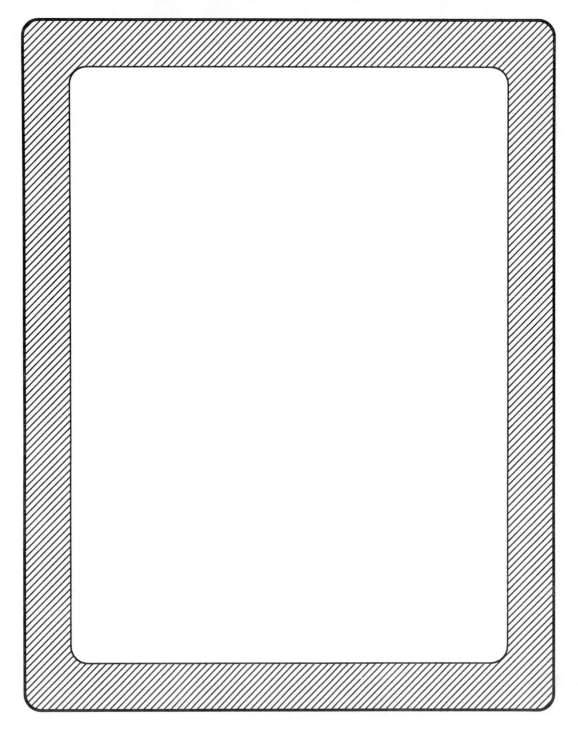

© COPYRIGHT, The Center for Learning. Used with permission. Not for resale.

Family History

Objectives

- To introduce genealogy
- To encourage family history research and investigate the relationship between family history and American history
- To learn about Abraham Lincoln's family history and understand its relationship to American history

Interdisciplinary Strands

English/Language Arts, Art, Geography

Notes to the Teacher

Students often do not think of history as a living subject. They view it as something that happened to other people long ago or as something that is happening now to the "rich and famous." Genealogy provides a way to bring history alive for students in an interesting personal way.

Students read selections from Abraham Lincoln's autobiography and family history facts from a standard reference book before reviewing a graphic presentation of the Lincoln family tree. Students interview family members, peruse pertinent documents, and combine the results of his research with their recollections, to write a brief family history and prepare a family tree leaf for the class family history tree. They should see their family and themselves as part of the general flow of American history.

Resources

1. Coolidge, Olivia. *The Apprenticeship of Abraham Lincoln*. New York: Charles Scribner's Sons, 1974.

2. D'Aulaire, Ingri and Edgar Parin. *Abraham Lincoln*. New York: Doubleday and Company, Inc., 1947.

3. Daughters, James. *Abraham Lincoln*. New York: The Viking Press, 1943.

4. Draznin, Yaffa. *The Family Historian's Handbook*. New York: Jane Publications, 1978.

5. The Editors of Consumer Guide. *Tracing Your Roots*. New York: Bell Publishing   Company, 1977.

6. Gilford, Henry. *Genealogy: How to Find Your Roots*. New York: Franklin Watts, 1978.

7. Provenzo, Eugene F. and Asterie Baker Provenzo, and Peter A. Zorn, Jr. *Pursuing the Past, Teacher's Handbook*. Menlo Park, Calif.: Addison-Wesley Publishing Company, 1984.

8. *Suggestions for Beginners in Genealogy*. Washington, D.C.: The National Genealogical Society, 1976.

MATERIALS:
Handouts 35 and 36, colored markers or crayons, cellophane tape, scissors

TERMS:
ancestor, autobiography, biography, conjecture, descendant, frontier, genealogy, lineage

Procedure

1. Ask why interest in family history has increased over the last decade. Answers will vary. Alex Haley's *Roots* will probably be mentioned as a catalyst for renewed interest in genealogy. Emphasize that family members and documents (interviews; birth, baptismal, marriage, and death certificates; baby books; diaries, scrapbooks; and family photo albums) are useful sources for genealogical research.

2. Use the terms and the discussion as springboards to the handouts. Clarify the difference between an ancestor and a descendant and between an autobiography and a biography. Explain the relationship of the terms to the study of family history.

3. Have students read **Handout 35**. Note that Lincoln's autobiographical sketch contained some family hearsay that was not correct. Emphasize the correlation between the Lincoln family's migration pattern and the moving western frontier. Trace their movements on a United States wall map. Help students see how the information given in the narratives appears on the visual display of Lincoln's family history.

4. Allow sufficient time for students to complete **Handout 36**. Family interviews and documents should be cited as sources.

5. Debrief by conducting a discussion which focuses on the process. Did information or facts differ in people's recollections? What documents were useful? How did your family history parallel American history? Did you have difficulty in moving the information from the narrative to a visual display? Answers will vary.

6. Have students prepare a bulletin board display of a tree trunk and branches. When students have colored and cut out their family tree leaves, tape them to the bulletin board to make a "Class Family History Tree."

Enrichment/Extension

1. Replicate the first part of the lesson. Have students select other American presidents or significant persons, read autobiographies/biographies, write their version of the biography, and prepare a leaf from the family tree of the subject.

2. Visit the local historical society and have the archivist explain how genealogical research is done with their collection.

3. Invite a person who has researched his/her family history to speak to the class on how the task was accomplished and what sources were used.

Social Studies Activities
U.S. History and Geography 1
Lesson 14
Handout 35 (page 1)—*Sample*

Name _____

Date _____

Abraham Lincoln's Autobiography

Abraham Lincoln wrote this family history in June 1860 as part of an autobiography he did to help writers who were preparing a biography for use in the presidential election campaign.

Abraham Lincoln was born Feb. 12, 1809, then in Hardin, now in the more recently formed county of Larue, Kentucky. His father, Thomas, & grand-father, Abraham, were born in Rockingham county Virginia, whither their ancestors had come from Berks county, Pennsylvania. His lineage has been traced no farther back than this. The family were originally quakers, though in later times they have fallen away from the peculiar habits of that people. The grand-father Abraham, had four brothers—Isaac, Jacob, John & Thomas. So far as known, the descendants of Jacob and John are still in Virginia. Isaac went to a place near where Virginia, North Carolina, and Tennessee, join; and his de[s]cendants are in that region. Thomas came to Kentucky, and after many years, died there, whence his de[s]cendants went to Missouri. Abraham, grandfather of the subject of this sketch, came to Kentucky, and was killed by indians about the year 1784. He left a widow, three sons and two daughters. The eldest son, Mordecai, remained in Kentucky till late in life, when he removed to Hancock county, Illinois, where soon after he died, and where several of his descendants still reside. The second son, Joshua, removed at an early day to a place on Blue River, now within Harrison [Hancock] county, Indiana; but no recent information of him, or his family, has been obtained. The eldest sister, Mary, married Ralph Crume and some of her descendants are now known to be in Breckinridge county Kentucky. The second sister, Nancy, married William Brumfield, and her family are not known to have left Kentucky, but there is no recent information from them. Thomas, the youngest son, and father of the present subject married Nancy Hanks— mother of the present subject—in the year 1706. She also was born in Virginia; and relatives of hers of the name of Hanks, and of other names, now reside in Coles, in Macon, and in Adams counties,

© COPYRIGHT, The Center for Learning. Used with permission. Not for resale.

Social Studies Activities
U.S. History and Geography 1
Lesson 14
Handout 35 (page 2)—*Sample*

Name _____

Date _____

Illinois, and also in Iowa. The present subject has no brother or sister of the whole or half blood. He had a sister, older than himself, who was grown and married, but died many years ago, leaving no child. Also a brother, younger than himself who died in infancy.[1]

---

[1] Ralph G. Newman, ed., *Lincoln for the Ages* (Garden City, N.Y.: Doubleday and Company, Inc., 1960), 36–37.

© COPYRIGHT, The Center for Learning. Used with permission. Not for resale.

Social Studies Activities
U.S. History and Geography 1
Lesson 14
Handout 35 (page 3)—*Sample*

Name _____

Date _____

Abraham Lincoln's Biography

The family history of Abraham Lincoln which follows is typical of those found in general reference works.

". . . research has disclosed a lineage reaching back to Samuel Lincoln who came from Hingham, England, and settled in Hingham, Mass., in 1637. On the Lincoln side the descent was as follows: Samuel Lincoln (d. 1690); Mordecai Lincoln of Hingham and Scituate, Mass. (d. 1727); Mordecai Lincoln of Berks County, Pa. (d. 1736); John Lincoln of Berks County, Pa. and Rockingham County, Va. (d. 1788); Abraham Lincoln of Rockingham County, Va. and later of Kentucky (d. 1786); Thomas Lincoln (d. 1851) father of the President."

. . . "Thomas' first wife, Nancy Hanks was the mother of Abraham. According to the best available authority, she was the natural child of Lucy Hanks; and her paternity is unknown, the date of her birth being a matter of conjecture. Some years after the birth of Nancy, Lucy Hanks married Henry Sparrow in Mercer County, Ky.; and Nancy was reared by her aunt, Betsy Hanks (Mrs. Thomas Sparrow)."

[1] Dumas Malone, ed. *Dictionary of American Biography*, Volume 11 (New York: Charles Scribner's Sons, 1933), 242.

© COPYRIGHT, The Center for Learning. Used with permission. Not for resale.

Name _____

Date _____

A Leaf from Abraham Lincoln's Family Tree

Mother   **Father**

Unknown
Great Great Grandfather

Mordecai Lincoln
Great Great Grandfather

Unknown
Great Great Grandmother

Hannah Browne
Great Great Grandmother

Unknown
Great Grandfather

John Lincoln
Great Grandfather

Unknown
Great Grandmother

Rebecca Flowers
Great Grandmother

Unknown
Grandfather

Abraham Lincoln
Grandfather

Lucy Hanks Sparrow
Grandmother

Bathsheba ?
Grandmother

Nancy Hanks
Mother

Thomas Lincoln
Father

Abraham Lincoln[1]

[1] Taken from Ralph G. Newman, ed., *Lincoln for the Ages* (Garden City, N.Y.: Doubleday and Company, Inc., 1960), 38–42.

© COPYRIGHT, The Center for Learning. Used with permission. Not for resale.

Name _____

Date _____

A Narrative of My Family History

_____

_____

_____

_____

_____

_____

_____

_____

_____

_____

_____

_____

_____

_____

_____

_____

_____

_____

_____

_____

_____

_____

Sources: _____

_____

_____

© COPYRIGHT, The Center for Learning. Used with permission. Not for resale.

Name _____

Date _____

A Leaf from My Family Tree

Mother   **Father**

Great Great Grandfather   Great Great Grandfather

Great Great Grandmother   Great Great Grandmother

Great Grandfather   Great Grandfather

Great Grandmother   Great Grandmother

Grandfather   Grandfather

Grandmother   Grandmother

Mother   Father

_____
(Your Name)

Sources: _____

_____

_____

© COPYRIGHT, The Center for Learning. Used with permission. Not for resale.

Divide and Reunite

Objectives

- To learn about the advantages and disadvantages of the North and South during the Civil War Era
- To practice using Venn Diagrams to compare contrast information and form hypotheses

Interdisciplinary Strands

English/Language Arts, Geography

Notes to the Teacher

Students need practice in categorizing information, making comparisons and contrasts, and reaching conclusions based on thoughtful consideration of data. This lesson utilizes Venn Diagrams to help students organize information relative to the advantages and disadvantages of both the North and South at the onset of the Civil War, how to compare and contrast their positions, and to formulate and defend a hypothesis on the eventual outcome of the conflict.

This lesson is designed to culminate a unit of study on the Civil War and reconstruction period. It helps students take notes and organize facts in a meaningful way.

MATERIALS:
Handouts 37 and 38, content books, U.S. wall map

TERMS:
antebellum, civil war, diagram, foreign war, Reconstruction, sectionalism

Resources

1. Beatty, Jerome. *Blockade.* New York: Doubleday and Company, 1971.

2. Catton, Bruce. *This Hollowed Ground.* New York: Doubleday and Company, 1965.

3. Fleming, Thomas. *Band of Brothers: West Point in the Civil War.* New York: Walker Publishing Company, Inc., 1988.

4. Hayman, Leroy. *The Road to Fort Sumter.* New York: Thomas Y. Crowell Company, 1972.

5. Katz, William Loren. *An Album of the Civil War.* New York: Franklin Watts, Inc., 1974.

6. Welsh, Douglas. *The Civil War.* Greenwich, Conn.: Bison Book Corp., 1982.

Procedure

1. Explain that the class is going to do some work on the Civil War and Reconstruction Era which will require working with information. Permit each student to bring to class and use *one* three-ring binder size sheet of notes. Notes may be written on both sides of the paper. No printed material will be permitted. Decide if the note taking is a homework or classwork assignment.

2. Review the basic facts concerning sectionalism. Locate the North, South, and West on a U.S. wall map and draw from the class brief descriptions of each section. Concentrate on the North and South, and stress the economic differences.

3. Divide the class into two groups, one representing the North and the other the South. Have each group compile a list of their advantages and disadvantages in case of war. Share the lists and seek consensus. Place the agreed upon advantages and disadvantages for each side on the chalkboard.

4. Have students compare their individual and consensus lists with those listed on **Handout 37**, page 1. Debrief the Venn diagram by noting that the categories are listed in the overlap of the circles. Have students decide if the items listed under the North/South circles are advantages or disadvantages for waging a war. The diagram is slanted so that advantages are listed for one side (North) and disadvantages are listed for the other side (South).

5. Using only the information on the handout, have students hypothesize if their group (North/South) will win or lose the coming war and why. Share the responses and reasoning.

6. Repeat the process for **Handout 37,** page 2. Again, categories are in the overlap. Make sure the students note that only one section (the South) is involved. The left circle is up to and during the Civil War; the right circle is during and immediately following Reconstruction. Have students compare their individual and consensus lists with the information listed and decide if the diagram could have been constructed from their notes.

7. Using only the information on the handout, have students hypothesize if the South was better or worse off after Civil War and Reconstruction and why. Share the responses and reasoning. Answers will vary.

8. Have students, individually or in small groups, and with only their notes for data, construct a Venn Diagram using **Handout 38**. They must select the categories for the overlap and complete the outlying circles appropriately. Share the completed diagrams.

Enrichment/Extension

1. Use the Venn Diagram technique to compare and contrast other subject content. For instance, the mining and farming frontiers, the boom (1920s) and bust (1930s) eras, or the face of Europe before and after World War I.

2. Practice note taking by distributing blank Venn Diagrams and having students use it to take/organize notes on their initial reading of subject content.

3. Use completed Venn Diagrams as outlines from which students develop a paragraph or essay about a selected topic.

Name _____

Date _____

North and South Before the Civil War

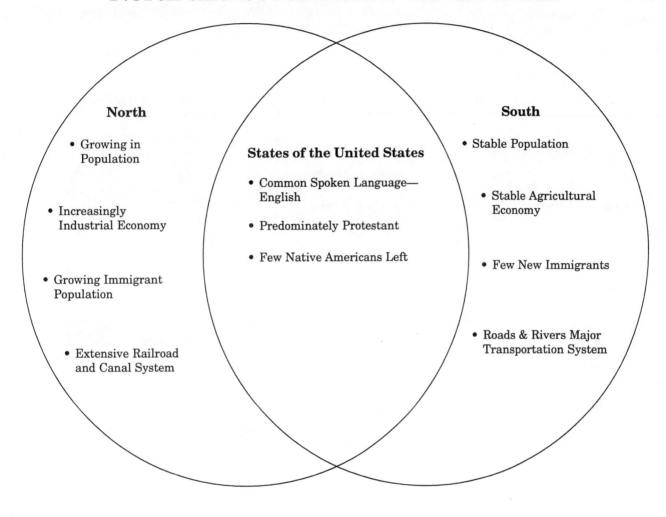

North

- Growing in Population

- Increasingly Industrial Economy

- Growing Immigrant Population

- Extensive Railroad and Canal System

States of the United States

- Common Spoken Language— English

- Predominately Protestant

- Few Native Americans Left

South

- Stable Population

- Stable Agricultural Economy

- Few New Immigrants

- Roads & Rivers Major Transportation System

© COPYRIGHT, The Center for Learning. Used with permission. Not for resale.

Name _____

Date _____

Before, During, and After the Civil War

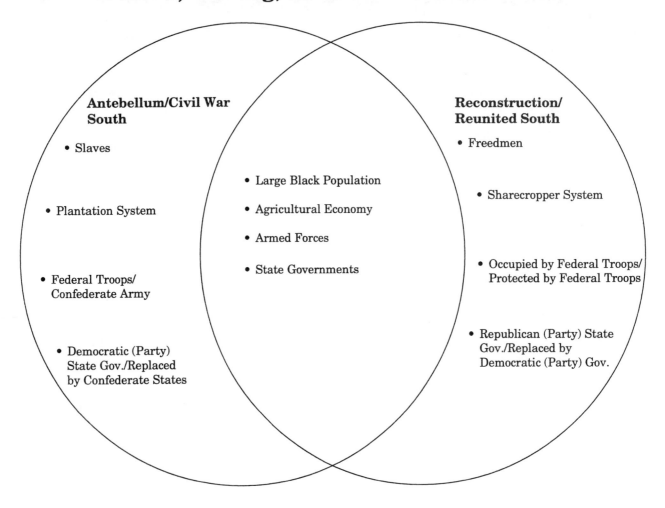

Antebellum/Civil War South

- Slaves

- Plantation System

- Federal Troops/ Confederate Army

- Democratic (Party) State Gov./Replaced by Confederate States

- Large Black Population
- Agricultural Economy
- Armed Forces
- State Governments

Reconstruction/ Reunited South

- Freedmen

- Sharecropper System

- Occupied by Federal Troops/ Protected by Federal Troops

- Republican (Party) State Gov./Replaced by Democratic (Party) Gov.

© COPYRIGHT, The Center for Learning. Used with permission. Not for resale.

Name _____

Date _____

Title of My Venn Diagram

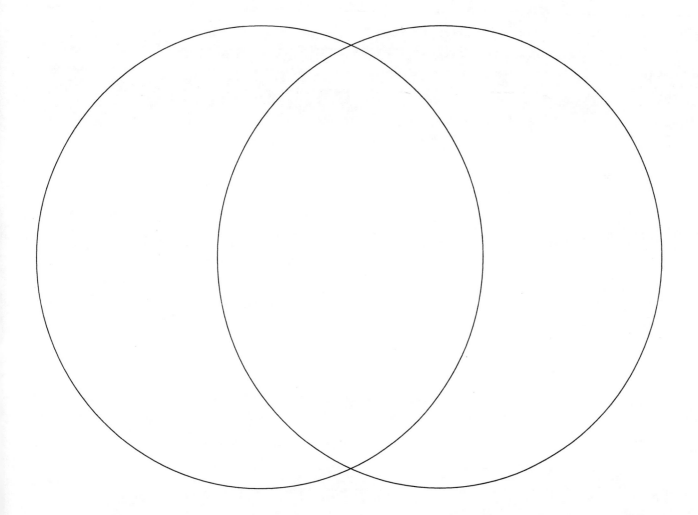

© COPYRIGHT, The Center for Learning. Used with permission. Not for resale.

Part IV

Geography

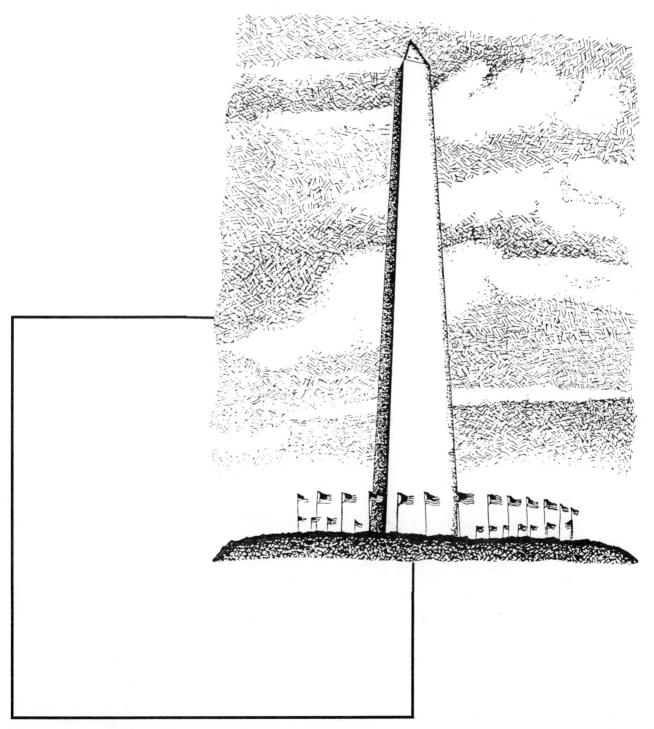

Washington, D.C.

Objectives

- To investigate the uniqueness of a national capital
- To learn about the capital of the United States, Washington, D.C.

Interdisciplinary Strands

Language Arts, Geography, Art

Notes to the Teacher

This lesson can be taught in chronological sequence, following the study of the compromise which prompted setting up the federal district as the site of the new nation's capital, or it can be taught as an independent instructional unit at any time during the course. It has a strong geography component and reinforces map reading skills.

There are many picture books on Washington and students should have no difficulty in locating examples to help them sketch the point of interest they select. Reassure them that the effort, not the technical expertise or artistic talent, is important. Consider allowing them to use copy machine reproductions if students continue to resist the sketching portion of the activity. Students who do sketches deserve special recognition.

MATERIALS:
Handouts 39 and 40, library books

TERMS:
capital, capitol, D.C., federal district, First Family, memorial, monument, site

Resources

1. Anglesworth, Thomas G. and Virginia L. *Let's Discover the States: Atlantic - District of Columbia, Virginia, West Virginia.* New York: Chelsea House Publishers, 1988.

2. Carpenter, Allan. *The New Enchantment of America: District of Columbia.* Chicago: Regensteiner Publishing Enterprises, Inc., 1979. Revised Edition.

3. Epstein, Sam and Beryl. *Washington, D. C. The Nation's Capital.* New York: Franklin Watts, 1981. A First Book/Revised Edition.

4. Fisher, Leonard Everett. *The White House.* New York: Holiday House, Inc., 1989.

5. Lumley, Kathryn Wentzel. *District of Columbia in Words and Pictures.* Chicago: Regensteiner Publishing Enterprises, Inc., 1981.

6. Phelan, Mary Kay. *The Burning of Washington: August 1814.* New York: Thomas Y. Crowell Company, 1975.

Procedures

1. Ask if anyone has visited Washington, D.C. If some students have been there, encourage them to share their experiences as an introduction to the lesson. A visual introduction (videotape, short film, or filmstrip) is an alternative.

2. Have students locate Washington, D.C., on wall maps of the world and the U.S. and on a globe.

3. Carefully review the map on page 1 of **Handout 39**. A transparency is an easy way to discuss the features on the map.

4. Conduct a brief oral quiz on the map. For instance, ask
   • What direction is the Pentagon from The White House? (southwest)
   • The Reflecting Pool is between which two points of interest? (The Lincoln Memorial and The Washington Monument)
   • What President's grave is shown on the map? (John F. Kennedy's)

   Do not continue until students understand how to read the map and can interpret it correctly.

5. After reading and discussing the remainder of **Handout 39**, help students analyze the selection as a piece of writing.
   • The first two paragraphs deal with its early history.
   • Paragraph three focuses on the ownership and uses of the facility.
   • The fourth paragraph provides "human interest" about use of The White House lawn.
   • The final paragraph tries to establish a link between the reader and the building.

6. Distribute **Handout 40**. Using their maps, have students select one point of interest to research and sketch. Have a sign-up sheet for student selections. Based on class size and resource material available, limit the number assigned to any one point of interest.

7. Have students share interesting facts they have unearthed on their topic by making oral presentations. Use the completed handouts for a bulletin board display. Finally, place copies in their *My American History Book.*

Enrichment/Extension

1. Have students research, draw, and report on important public buildings and monuments in their state and community.

2. Replicate the activity for other national capitals around the world.

Name _____

Date _____

Map of Washington, D.C.

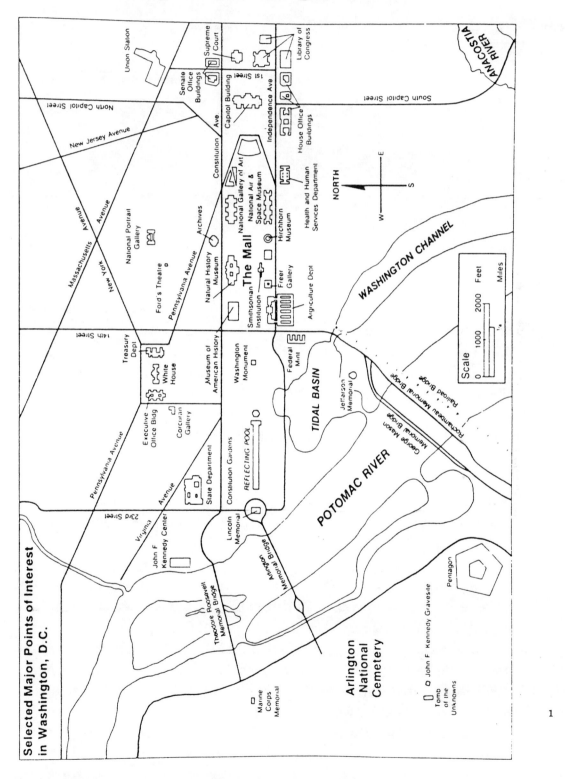

[1] Adapted from Herbert H. Gross, *World Geography Workbook* (Newton, Mass. Allyn and Bacon, Inc., 1986), 143.

© COPYRIGHT, The Center for Learning. Used with permission. Not for resale.

Name _____

Date _____

Our Nation's Capital—The White House

Drawing

Report:

The White House, home of the President of the United States, is located in Washington, D.C. at 1600 Pennsylvania Avenue. The site was chosen by George Washington although he never got to live there. In fact, it was still unfinished when John Adams, the second president, and his family moved in. They used what is now the East Room as a drying room for their laundry!

By the time the fourth president, James Madison, and his wife, Dolley, moved in, the house was completed. The British promptly burned it down in a military campaign which was part of the War of 1812. Reconstruction included painting the formerly yellow house white in order to conceal fire damage. It soon became known as The White House.

The White House is the property of the American people. The president lives there while in office and moves out when the next person elected president moves in. The Oval Office, the work place of the president, is located in The White House. There is an area open to the public with tours available. Another area is the private residence of the First Family. Over the years The White House has hosted births, deaths, weddings, formal state dinners, lawn parties, and a variety of family pets.

© COPYRIGHT, The Center for Learning. Used with permission. Not for resale.

Social Studies Activities
U.S. History and Geography 1
Lesson 16
Handout 39 (page 3)—*Sample*

Name _____

Date _____

Lincoln's boys rode their ponies on the lawn. William Howard Taft practiced his favorite game, golf, there. Lyndon Baines Johnson, to the delight of the Washington press corps, exercised his hunting dogs regularly. George Bush installed horseshoe courts. The Rose Garden is often used for award ceremonies and picture opportunities. The helicopter pad, a relatively recent addition, is as busy a place as the stables and garages used to be.

Inside and out, The White House is an interesting place to read about and/or visit. It is important to the nation and also plays a vital role in international affairs. Do you know who lives in The White House now?

© COPYRIGHT, The Center for Learning. Used with permission. Not for resale.

Name _____

Date _____

Our Nation's Capital_____

Drawing:

Source:

_____

_____

© COPYRIGHT, The Center for Learning. Used with permission. Not for resale.

Name _____

Date _____

Our Nation's Capital_____

Report:

_____

_____

_____

_____

_____

_____

_____

_____

_____

_____

_____

_____

_____

_____

_____

_____

_____

_____

_____

_____

_____

_____

Source:

_____

_____

© COPYRIGHT, The Center for Learning. Used with permission. Not for resale.

The Local Area

Objectives

- To study the geography of the local area
- To increase understanding of a variety of geographical concepts
- To increase interest in regional geography

Interdisciplinary Strands

English/Language Arts, Art, Geography, Math, Science

Notes to the Teacher

United States geography is difficult for students because they approach it with a limited experience base. Many haven't traveled extensively and they don't know much about their own local area, let alone their region. This lesson helps expand students' understanding of their own area. It provides a springboard to study the other regions of the country.

If another teacher gives a similar assignment, exchange the resulting booklets. Doing this motivates students to complete their handouts more carefully.

Students may be confused by the use of the term "area" in this lesson. In many cases, substituting "city" would convey the size of unit intended for this lesson— the city plus its surrounding hinterland. For those living in rural areas, "area" may need to be translated as "township" or "county."

A good map of the area is needed. City maps are generally easy to find. The Chamber of Commerce usually can provide one. Topographic maps from the U.S. Geological Survey are very attractive, stimulating, and inexpensive. Often, they can be purchased locally from sporting stores, map stores, or state governments (try the department of natural resources). They can also be ordered by contacting:

National Cartographic Information Center
U.S. Geological Survey
507 National Center
Reston, VA 22092
(703) 860-6045

MATERIALS:
Handouts 41 and 42; copies of a local map, telephone books, and classified ads from a local newspaper; rulers; colored pencils; and fine-tip colored markers

TERMS:
domestic, foreign, population density, topography

Procedure

1. Locate the local area on a state map, a U.S. map, a world map, and a globe.

2. Before working on **Handout 41**, have students look at maps of the local area and discuss their features. Prepare students to make maps by helping them decide what information will go on their map and what will be omitted. If possible, provide each one with a copy of a local map to use as a guide. Encourage students to color the maps and use completed maps for a bulletin board display.

3. Have students bring in telephone books and copies of the local newspaper. Collect other useful references—real estate booklets, business directories, and other printed materials available from shopping mall offices, the Chamber of Commerce and similar community organizations—and have them available for students.

4. Review **Handout 42** item-by-item. Discuss how to determine an average of housing costs or apartment rentals. Discuss how to use the Yellow Pages and give hints on where to find the other kinds of information requested. Actual postcards can be shown as examples for page 6.

5. Debrief the activity by having students share and compare their responses throughout the handout. Tally the class response on the chalkboard. Reach consensus on the category that best fits the local area.

6. Lead a discussion about the local area and what makes it special. Some questions that might be good initiators:
   * If others used our projects to judge our area, how would we fare?
   * In what ways is our area typical of our region? Are we typically Southern or Midwestern?
   * How do the different aspects of our area relate to each other?
   * How does the climate affect our main products?
   * How do the landforms affect our transportation linkages?
   * What is the impact of our population density?

   Help students analyze the local area in terms of its relationship to regional, national, and global situations.

Enrichment/Extension

1. Arrange for a realtor, city official, or person from the convention bureau/chamber of commerce to speak to the class about the local area and how they "sell" it to visitors and newcomers.

2. Replicate the activity by completing the handouts for another area. The new area could be in another region of the United States or anywhere in the world.

Name _____

Date _____

My Map of Our Area

Directions: Make a simple map of our area. Include the main land and water forms, the main highways, the main shopping areas, important buildings, the school, and your residence. Make sure your map has the following: title, legend, compass rose, and scale indicator.

© COPYRIGHT, The Center for Learning. Used with permission. Not for resale.

Social Studies Activities
U.S. History and Geography 1
Lesson 17
Handout 42 (page 1)

Name _____

Date _____

Instruction Sheet for "The Real Story"

page 2

Location in the State:

Draw the outline of our state and place a star on our area's location.

Population Density:

Find our area's population density and write it in. Put one dot for each *person per square mile.*

Fun Things to Do:

Draw pictures of some of the fun activities of our area.

Main Products:

Draw and label pictures of our area's main products.

page 3

Housing Costs:

Use newspaper ads or booklets from local realtors to figure average costs for these three kinds of housing.

Changes:

List three ways this area has been getting better in the middle portion of the sheet. On the bottom, list two ways the area has been getting worse.

page 4

Car Dealers:

List the makes of cars that have dealerships locally. Place American carmakers on the left and foreign carmakers on the right.

FM Radio Stations:

List two or three best FM radio stations as shown:

| 88 | 92 | 100 | 104 | 108 |

93.2 WWAX
Country &
Western

105.9 WFIB
Top 40 Rock

page 5

Checklist

Use the telephone book to decide whether to check yes or no on each of the items listed.

page 6

Postcard

Front—Select something that represents our area (famous person, building; local industry, local tourist attraction) and draw it in.

Back—Write a postcard that a visitor might send home describing his/her stay in our area. Use the proper form for both the message and address sides.

© COPYRIGHT, The Center for Learning. Used with permission. Not for resale.

Social Studies Activities
U.S. History and Geography 1
Lesson 17
Handout 42 (page 2)

Name _____

Date _____

Our Area: The Real Story

Name of our area:_____ Our state:_____

Location in the State	**Population Density**
	U.S. average=**69** people per square mile Our area=____ people per square mile
Fun Things to Do	**Main Products**

© COPYRIGHT, The Center for Learning. Used with permission. Not for resale.

Name _____

Date _____

Our Area: The Real Story

$ Housing Costs $

Average cost of a
NEW home.

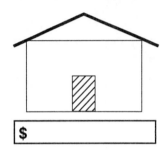

Average cost of an
OLDER home.

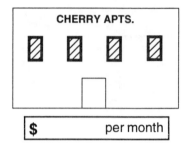

Average rent for a
two-bedroom
apartment.

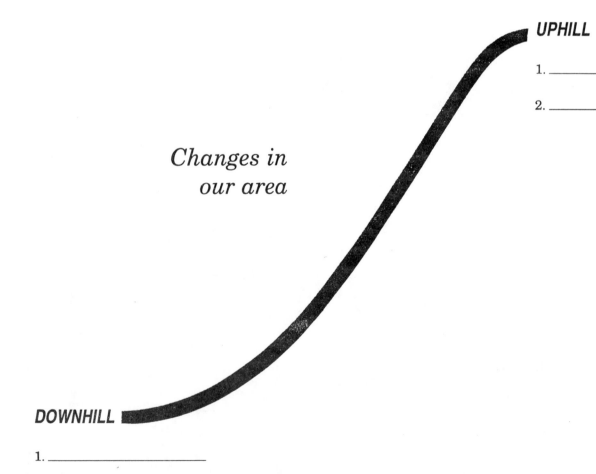

*Changes in
our area*

UPHILL

1. _____

2. _____

DOWNHILL

1. _____

2. _____

© COPYRIGHT, The Center for Learning. Used with permission. Not for resale.

Social Studies Activities
U.S. History and Geography 1
Lesson 17
Handout 42 (page 4)

Name _____

Date _____

Our Area: The Real Story

Car Dealers

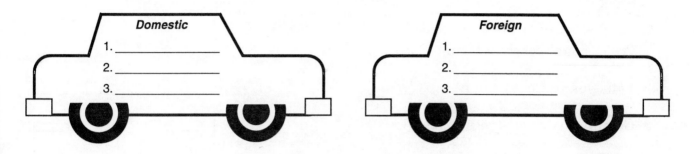

Domestic	Foreign
1. _____	1. _____
2. _____	2. _____
3. _____	3. _____

Best FM Radio Stations

88	92	100	104	108

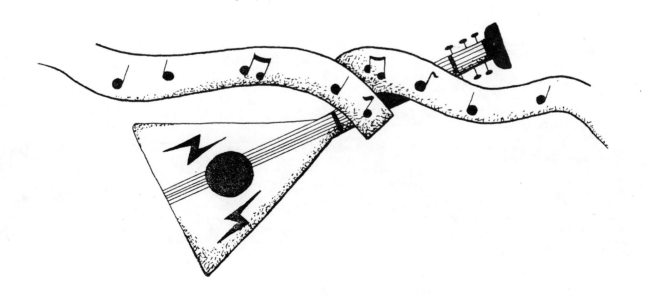

© COPYRIGHT, The Center for Learning. Used with permission. Not for resale.

Name _____

Date _____

Our Area: The Real Story

Does our area have a (an) . . .

	YES	NO
1. Professional baseball team?		
2. Four-year college or university?		
3. Community or business college?		
4. Zoo? (Schools don't count.)		
5. Museum (historical or science)?		
6. Shopping mall?		
7. Flush toilets?		
8. Airport?		
9. Drug-crisis hotline?		
10. Real estate office?		
11. U.S. Congressional Office?		
12. U.S. Post Office		
13. Restaurant that delivers pizza?		
14. Fresh fish market?		
15. Chinese restaurant?		

s c o r e

12–15	Yes—Big City
8–11	Yes—Medium City
4–7	Yes—Small Town
0–3	Yes—The Sticks

© COPYRIGHT, The Center for Learning. Used with permission. Not for resale.

Name _____

Date _____

Our Area: The Real Story

Post Card

State Data

Objectives

- To learn about the states
- To evaluate the importance of different kinds of information
- To appreciate the use of computers

Interdisciplinary Strands

Art, Computer Education, Geography, Science

Notes to the Teacher

This lesson is an attempt to interest students in comparative information about the states. It begins with some number one producers' data that they can relate to—Florida for oranges, North Carolina for tobacco. They then make a map reflecting this information, which gives them additional practice in locating the states. Students do an activity which helps them think about how one might use statistics normally associated with the states. Finally, they do some simple research on the states and play a simple game, "Human Data Base." This last activity helps them understand computer data bases.

The desire to list a number one producer designation for each state resulted in the use of some relatively obscure products. Therefore, a glossary is included.

Handout 45 presents most of the categories of information provided for each state by *The World Almanac and Book of Facts*. This handout asks students to consider which categories they would use to make certain kinds of decisions. The last column was left unlabeled so a category of choice can be added. It is best for students to consider these questions before they see any of the specific data for a state. **Handout 45** also provides a blank page of this data for students to flesh out for assigned states.

The lesson concludes with a learning activity about computer data bases. The way a data base works is that questions can be asked about any field of information on the page. For example, a computer user can move the cursor to the topography field and ask the computer to call up all of the states that have the word "mountains" in them. Or it can go to the population density field and ask to see all of the states with fewer than ten people per square mile. A data base can also record all of the pages on the basis of any field. For example, in a few seconds, the states can be put in order (from most to least or vice versa) of population size, of income per person, or other categories. By having students make signs to wear identifying which state they represent, these computer data bases can be recreated in a number of ways. Depending on the questions, some commotion may occur as students consult with each other and put themselves in the proper order. It is a good learning exercise despite the disruption possibility because it provides a practical demonstration of how a computer data base works.

One important outcome of this lesson is to get students to think about facts and help them realize that there is more information available about the states than they can remember. It emphasizes that learning how to look data up and use it properly is as important as remembering things. With today's information explosion, research skills and knowledge of computers are increasingly necessary.

MATERIALS:
Handouts 43, 44, and 45; copies of reference books, especially almanacs, colored pencils or markers; art materials for sign making; U.S. wall map.

TERMS:
climate, topography, data base, all the products listed in the glossary

Resources

1. Hoffman, Mark S., ed. *The World Almanac and Book of Facts 1989.* New York: Newspaper Enterprise Association, Inc.
   Information Please Almanac. New York: Simon and Schuster, 1990.

2. National Geographic Society. *Our Fifty States.* Washington, D.C.: National Geographic Society, 1980.

3. U.S. Department of Commerce. *Statistical Abstract of the United States 1989.* Washington, D.C.: U.S. Government Printing Office, 1989.

Procedure

1. Ask students if they know what their state is the number one producer of. List responses on the chalkboard. Answers will vary. Once the list is complete, circle the correct response. Quiz them on a few other number one designations: which state is number one in the production of pineapples? (Hawaii) Gold? (Nevada)

2. Use **Handout 43** to help students discover which states are the number one producers of various products. As the information is reviewed, locate the states on a U.S. wall map. Note the influence of geography on the products—plain states tend to have agricultural products while mountainous states tend to have mineral products. The type of agricultural product is influenced by the climate—Idaho grows potatoes and Hawaii produces pineapples—and location—Maine could not produce Nebraska's seed corn volume and Nebraska's interior location makes sea coast Maine's lobsters impossible. Tell students to use the glossary in case they are not up on their animal, vegetable, and mineral resources from their science studies. Offer extra points to any student who can complete the listing and find number one products for those states left blank. Require them to document the reference book in which they find the information.

3. Help the class design appropriate symbols for each category. Some suggestions: cow for animal, potato for vegetable, and crossed pick and shovel for mineral. On **Handout 44**, have students place the correct symbol and write beneath it the number one product of each state listed. Color the maps and

use them for a classroom display.

4. Talk to the class about the value of these number one designations. Ask what other information would be good to know about each state. Make a list on the chalkboard of the responses. Compare the class list with the sixteen items listed on **Handout 45** page 1. Note that the fourth column has been left for the class and/or teacher to designate a category of interest. After students have completed the handout, share and compare responses. Conduct a discussion which focuses on what is worth knowing about the states and how data is used for different purposes.

5. Assign each student two or more states depending on the class size. Provide the necessary number of copies of **Handout 45**, page 2 for each student. Assign completion of the handout as classwork or as homework. Students will need reference books. Almanacs are especially useful.

6. When the work is completed, play "Human Data Base." Have students make and wear state signs for their assigned states. Encourage creative signs. Ask a variety of questions and have them refer to their pages, stand, and respond when appropriate. Make sure that every student gets to be involved. Debrief by discussing how a computer data base on the states works. The Notes to the Teacher provides information. A demonstration in a computer lab is ideal. Students can set up the data base using the categories from **Handout 45** and key in their research information. If one computer is available for whole group instruction, a commercial software data base on the states can be used for demonstration.

Enrichment/Extension

1. Practice writing business letters by having students use the addresses in their almanac to send for additional information about each of their assigned states.

2. Replicate the data base activity by applying it to other social studies content.

Name _____

Date _____

Number One Products

This State is the #1 Producer Of . . .

Alabama	—
Alaska	Tin
Arizona	Copper
Arkansas	Broilers*, bauxite
California	Manufacturing, vegetables
Colorado	Molybedenum*
Connecticut	—
Delaware	Marl*
Florida	Oranges, grapefruit
Georgia	Peanuts
Hawaii	Pineapples
Idaho	Potatoes, silver
Illinois	Pumpkins
Indiana	Popcorn
Iowa	Pigs, feed corn
Kansas	Wheat
Kentucky	Bituminous coal
Louisiana	Fish
Maine	Lobster
Maryland	Oysters

*Explained in glossary

© COPYRIGHT, The Center for Learning. Used with permission. Not for resale.

Social Studies Activities
U.S. History and Geography 1
Lesson 18
Handout 43 (page 2)—*Sample*

Name _____

Date _____

Massachusetts	Cranberries
Michigan	Automobiles, cherries
Minnesota	Iron, wild rice
Mississippi	Catfish
Missouri	Lead
Montana	Talc*
Nebraska	Seed corn
Nevada	Gold
New Hampshire	—
New Jersey	Salt hay*
New Mexico	Uranium
New York	Publishing
North Carolina	Tobacco, furniture
North Dakota	Sunflower seeds
Ohio	Greenhouse vegetables
Oklahoma	Mung beans*
Oregon	nickel, sawtimber
Pennsylvania	Anthracite coal, chocolate
Rhode Island	Lace

*Explained in glossary

© COPYRIGHT, The Center for Learning. Used with permission. Not for resale.

Social Studies Activities
U.S. History and Geography 1
Lesson 18
Handout 43 (page 3)—*Sample*

Name _____

Date _____

South Carolina	Manganese ore*
South Dakota	Geese, oats
Tennessee	Mules, zinc*
Texas	Beef cattle, oil, natural gas
Utah	—
Vermont	Maple sugar
Virginia	Blue crabs
Washington	Apples, raspberries
West Virginia	—
Wisconsin	Hay, dairy products
Wyoming	Sodium carbonate*

*Explained in glossary

© COPYRIGHT, The Center for Learning. Used with permission. Not for resale.

Social Studies Activities
U.S. History and Geography 1
Lesson 18
Handout 43 (page 4)—*Sample*

Name _____

Date _____

Glossary for Number One Products

Here are explanations for some of the state products that you may not recognize:

Bauxite—a mineral which is used to make aluminum

Broilers—chickens that are fed a high-energy diet and then slaughtered for their meat at about 7 weeks of age

Manganese—a silver-gray metal used in the production of steel

Marl—a layered rock used in making cement and fertilizer

Molybedenum—a mineral used to make special kinds of steel, like in x-ray lamps

Mung beans—a bean grown mostly in Asia. Its seeds are cooked or are eaten raw in salads

Salt hay—hay made from shore grasses and used as a protective mulch by gardeners

Sodium carbonate—also known as soda ash. This chemical is used in making glass, soap, and paper.

Tal—a white mineral used in making ceramic tiles and talcum powder

Zinc—a bluish-white metal used in making batteries, brass, and bronze.[1]

---

[1] Adapted from *The World Book Encyclopedia* (Chicago: World Book, Inc., 1987).

© COPYRIGHT, The Center for Learning. Used with permission. Not for resale.

Social Studies Activities
U.S. History and Geography 1
Lesson 18
Handout 44

Name _____

Date _____

United States (Including Alaska and Hawaii)

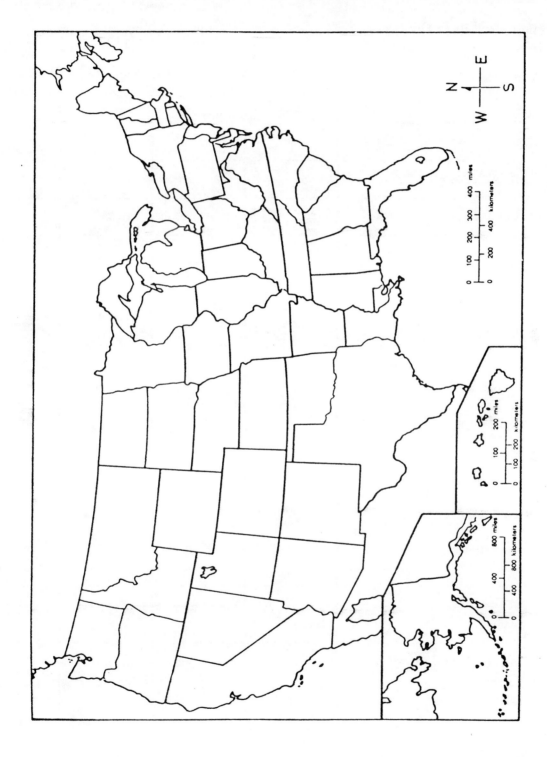

2

[2] Adapted from *Merrill Social Studies: Outline Map Resource Book* (Columbus, Ohio: Charles E. Merrill Publishing Company, 1986), 6.

© COPYRIGHT, The Center for Learning. Used with permission. Not for resale.

167

Social Studies Activities
U.S. History and Geography 1
Lesson 18
Handout 45 (page 1)

Name _____

Date _____

State Data: What's Important?

In each column, check the types of state information you would want to consult in order to decide . . .

	Where you want to live	Which state you want to visit	Where to build a factory	
1. Population				
2. Population density				
3. Growth or fall of population				
4. Size of the state (land area)				
5. Topography (hills, plains, etc.)				
6. Climate				
7. Economy (main products)				
8. History				
9. Income per person				
10. Unemployment rate				
11. Money spent for education				
12. Tourist attractions				
13. State bird				
14. State flower				
15. When entered the Union				
16. State capital[3]				

[3] Categories taken from *The World Almanac and Book of Facts 1989* (New York: World Almanac, 1989), 601–625.

© COPYRIGHT, The Center for Learning. Used with permission. Not for resale.

Social Studies Activities
U.S. History and Geography 1
Lesson 18
Handout 45 (page 2)

Name _____

Date _____

Making a States Data Base

┌─────────────────────────────┐
│   │
│   │
└─────────────────────────────┘

1. Population	
2. Population density	
3. Growth or fall of population	
4. Size of the state (land area)	
5. Topography (mountains, plains)	
6. Climate	
7. Economy (main products)	
8. History	
9. Income per person	
10. Unemployment rate	
11. Money spent for education	
12. Tourist attractions	
13. State bird	
14. State flower	
15. When entered the Union	
16. State capital[4]	

[4] Ibid.

© COPYRIGHT, The Center for Learning. Used with permission. Not for resale.

Climate

Objectives

- To read and interpret climate graphs
- To compare and contrast climates

Interdisciplinary Strands

English/Language Arts, Career Education, Math, Science

Notes to the Teacher

Many students do not have a sense of climate differences from one part of the United States to the other. This lesson can help fill that knowledge gap and can give students practice in making, reading, and interpreting graphs.

Handout 46 present graphs of the average monthly temperatures and precipitation for San Francisco and Detroit. San Francisco, like most of the West Coast, has a Mediterranean type climate. This is also called a subtropical dry-summer climate. Because of the ocean's influence, this is a moderate climate: warmer in the winter and cooler in the summer than inland areas. The precipitation patterns are markedly seasonal, with a rainy season in the late fall and winter months and a drought in the summer. A good stimulus to discussing San Francisco is Mark Twain's that the coldest winter he ever spent was a summer in San Francisco! Students might also be surprised to learn that people in the San Francisco Bay area do not normally swim much in the ocean. The water is too cold.

Detroit, on the other hand, has a decidedly continental climate which is known as humid cold. Like most of the Midwest and Northeast, Michigan is a battleground between polar and tropical air masses. The results are extremes of temperature and steady monthly amounts of precipitation. Detroit's proximity to the Great Lakes has little or no moderating influence on its climate. The last few pages of the exercise help students interpret the graphs by responding to a series of questions.

Handout 47 has students replicate the exercise by selecting a city, researching its average annual temperature and precipitation, and graphing the information. For temperatures, most sources give two statistics for a given month—average daily minimums and maximums. Have students take the average of the two numbers for use on their graphs. The lesson concludes with a discussion of climate and its affect on everyday life.

MATERIALS:
Handouts 46 and 47, wall map of the United States

TERMS:
climate, meteorologist, precipitation, temperature, weather, weatherman

Resources

1. Patton, Clyde P., Charles S. Alexander, and Fritz L. Kramer. *Physical Geography*. Belmont, Calif.: Wadsworth Publishing Company, Inc., 1970.

2. Pearce, E.A., and C. G. Smith. *World Weather Guide*. New York: Times Books, 1984.

3. *National Weather Service*—usually located at the nearest airport

4. Meteorologist/weatherman working at local television stations

Procedure

1. Ask students what the difference is between *weather* and *climate*. (Weather is short-term and climate is long-term.) Ask what the weather is where they live? The climate? Answers will vary depending on location.

2. Write *Detroit* and *San Francisco* on the chalkboard. Have students locate these cities on a U. S. wall map. Ask students to write a short paragraph in which they describe what they think the weather and climate are like in these cities. Read and compare student descriptions. Check the weather in each city by using the weather section of a current newspaper. *USA Today* has an outstanding weather section with excellent weather maps. Use pages 1 and 2 of **Handout 46** to obtain the climate information for the cities. By show of hands, determine how many of the students were "close" in their weather and climate descriptions for Detroit and San Francisco. Share information on the cities from the Notes to the Teacher.

3. Discuss the graphs. Ask students what the letters at the bottom of the graphs stand for. (They represent the twelve months of the year in order.) Remind them that water freezes at 32 degrees Fahrenheit. By keeping this in mind, they can read an average monthly temperature and make a good prediction of whether or not a place gets snow in that month.

4. Check on students ability to read the graphs by having them complete the remainder of **Handout 46**. Review the correct responses.

   Suggested Responses, Handout 46:

   Part One
   1. a. *September*   b. *July*   c. *Detroit*
         October   *August*
   2. a. *Around 50*   b. *San Francisco*
      b. *Around 25*
   3. *There is little seasonal varation in temperature.*

Part Two

4. a. 4 inches   b. 0 inches
     2 inches   3 inches

5. a. June   b. December   c. No
     July   January
     August   February

Part Three

6. Answers will vary.
7. a. Detroit   b. San Francisco   c. Detroit   d. Detroit

5. Discuss the factors that account for the differences in temperature and precipitation patterns. For example, one is located on the coast of a major ocean while the other is inland; one is located where Arctic blasts meet tropical air currents, the other is not. Ask students which of the two cities they would like to live in. Answers will vary.

6. Inform students that they are not limited to Detroit and San Francisco. Have them write the name of any American city in which they would like to live—excluding Detroit and San Francisco; permit no more than two students to select the city in which the class is located. Have students write the name of their selected city in the block at the top of **Handout 47**, page 1. Using reference books have students fill in the temperature and precipitation information. In case the school is situated in a rural area or if students want to live in a rural area, have them use statistics for the nearest city. Monitor students and provide assistance as needed.

7. Have students exchange completed graphs. Distribute **Handout 47**, page 2 and have students complete it using their peer's completed graphs. Form pairs and review correct responses. Answers will vary.

8. Conclude the activity by locating on a U.S. wall map the cities chosen. Conduct a discussion which focuses on such questions as: How does weather/climate affect what people wear? (If it rains, one uses an umbrella; changing seasons means two wardrobes.) How are houses built? (Adobe is popular in desert areas; saltbox houses with their steep roofs are practical in snowy New England.) What kinds of jobs are weather related? (Vertical climates often mean ski-related occupations and salt mines production helps keep road clear in winter.) Do not neglect to mention that being a weatherman or meteorologist is a viable career choice.

Enrichment/Extension

1. Provide data for the local area and have students graph it. This information can be taken from the *World Weather Guide* or similar reference books.

2. Have students make up what they consider the perfect climate—a climate for their dream city or location. Have them write a brief description of the climate and give their city a name which can serve as the title at the top of the page. At the bottom of the page, have students draw a leisure activity they would take part in. These could be done on poster board and used for classroom display.

3. Invite a meteorologist to speak to the class.

4. Use the weather page from *USA Today* and take the first few minutes of class for a report from a student designated as "Meteorologist-For-The-Day." Have a weather corner where the page is posted daily.

Name _____

Date _____

Temperature Graphs

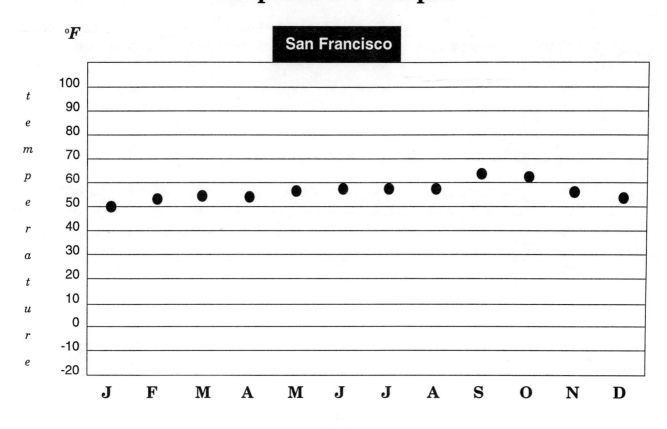

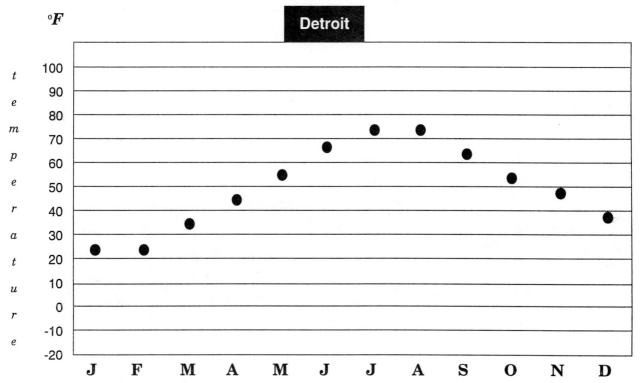

[1] E.A. Pearce and C.G. Smith, *World Weather Guide* (New York: Times Books, 1984), 138, 156.

© COPYRIGHT, The Center for Learning. Used with permission. Not for resale.

Name _____

Date _____

Precipitation Graphs

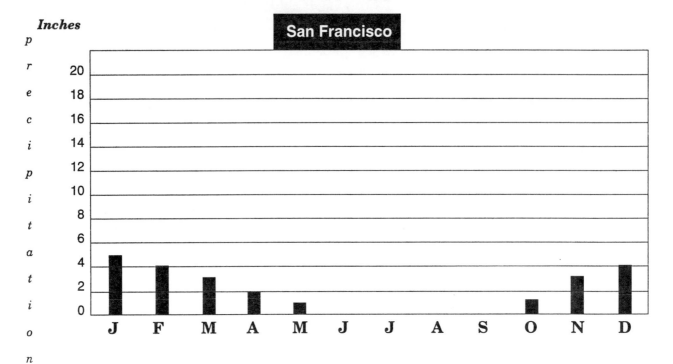

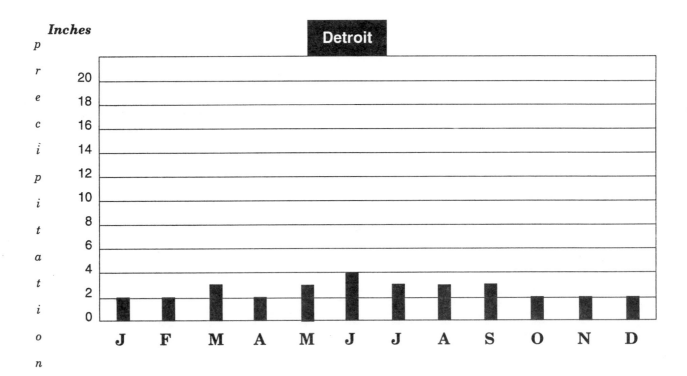

[2] Ibid.

© COPYRIGHT, The Center for Learning. Used with permission. Not for resale.

Social Studies Activities
U.S. History and Geography 1
Lesson 19
Handout 46 (page 3)—*Sample*

Name _____

Date _____

Reading Climate Graphs

Part One: Temperatures. Use page 1 of **Handout 46** to answer these questions about the climates of San Francisco.

    1. a. What are the two hottest months in San Francisco?

           _____   _____

        b. What are the two hottest months in Detroit?

           _____   _____

        c. Which city gets the hottest in the summer?_____

    2. a. What is the average January temperature for each city?
           San Francisco: _____   Detroit: _____

        b. Which of these cities almost never has snow?

           _____

    3. If you connected the dots on the San Francisco graph, it would form a nearly straight line. What does this tell you about the season in San Francisco?

        _____

Part Two: Precipitation. Answer these questions by using page 2 of **Handout 46**.

    4. a. How much precipitation does each city receive in February?
           San Francisco: _____   Detroit: _____

        b. How much does each receive in July?
           San Francisco: _____   Detroit: _____

    5. a. During which three months is there a dry season in San Francisco?

           _____ _____ _____

© COPYRIGHT, The Center for Learning. Used with permission. Not for resale.

Social Studies Activities
U.S. History and Geography 1
Lesson 19
Handout 46 (page 4)

Name _____

Date _____

b. During which three months is there a rainy season?

_____ _____ _____

c. Does Detroit have a wet season and a dry season?_____

Part Three: Putting It All Together. Use both handouts to answer these questions.

6. a. Which two climates do you prefer? (circle one)
   San Francisco   Detroit

   b. Why? _____

   _____

7. Which of these two cities would be a better place for each of these activities?

   a. Snowmobiling?_____

   b. Summer bike rides?_____

   c. Summer farming without irrigation?_____

   d. Fall color tours?_____

© COPYRIGHT, The Center for Learning. Used with permission. Not for resale.

Name _____

Date _____

Making Climate Graphs

Use the information on the right to make a temperature and a precipitation graph for this city.

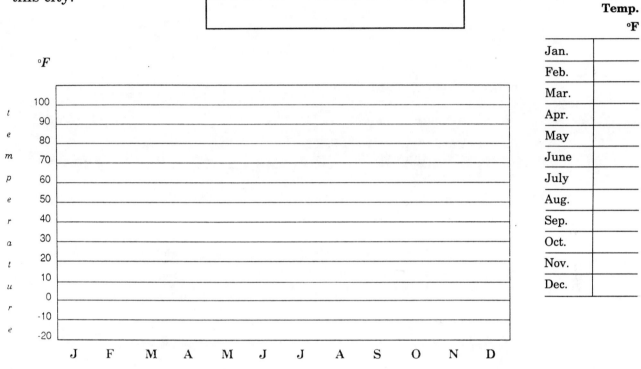

	Temp. °F
Jan.	
Feb.	
Mar.	
Apr.	
May	
June	
July	
Aug.	
Sep.	
Oct.	
Nov.	
Dec.	

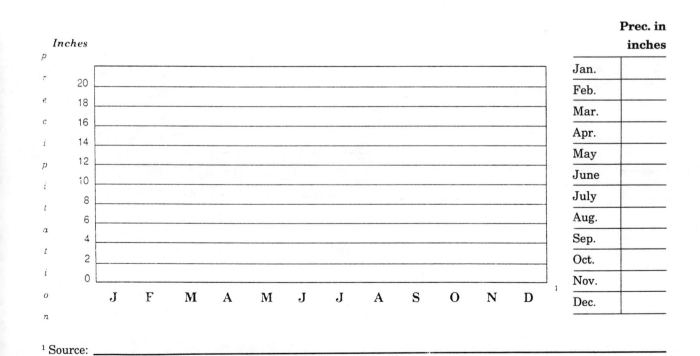

	Prec. in inches
Jan.	
Feb.	
Mar.	
Apr.	
May	
June	
July	
Aug.	
Sep.	
Oct.	
Nov.	
Dec.	

[1] Source: _____

© COPYRIGHT, The Center for Learning. Used with permission. Not for resale.

Social Studies Activities
U.S. History and Geography 1
Lesson 19
Handout 47 (page 2)

Name _____

Date _____

Interpreting Your Climate Graph

Use your graphs on **Handout 47** to complete these exercises:

1. Does this city have a wet season and a dry season? (circle one)
   YES   NO

2. a. Does it get snow during part of the year?   YES   NO

   b. If yes, during what months? _____
   _____

3. a. What are their summer temperatures like? (Circle one)
   HOT   WARM   COOL

   b. What are their winter temperatures like?
   WARM   COOL   COLD

4. In the spaces below, draw sketches of what children do outside during summer and winter in this area.

SUMMER   **WINTER**

© COPYRIGHT, The Center for Learning. Used with permission. Not for resale.

■

Tornadoes

Objectives

- To understand the distribution of tornadoes
- To discern patterns of data displayed on a map
- To learn tornado safety rules

Interdisciplinary Strands

English/Language Arts, Art, Geography, Science, Health and Safety

Notes to the Teacher

This lesson analyzes the distribution of data displayed on a map. It requires students to transfer data from one form to another. It is also an opportunity to review tornado safety rules if the school is located in a tornado-prone area.

The beginning of **Handout 48** presents the average number of tornadoes per year for each of the fifty states in chart form. Students are asked to transfer the statistics to a map on the next page. This provides additional practice in locating the states. A legend is provided that contains an interval of 15 (from 0–15, 16–31, etc.). The last page of **Handout 48** has two parts. The top half asks students to formulate generalizations based on their completed, color-coded maps. They are looking for the patterns illustrated by their maps. The maps and the diagram at the bottom of the page help students formulate generalizations.

Tornadoes are an outgrowth of thunderstorms. There are more tornadoes in the central United States than anywhere else in the world because of the peculiar topography of that region. Essentially, tornadoes are spawned when cold, dry air flowing above moves at right angles to surface winds that are hot and humid. The jet stream flowing across the Rockies provides the dry, upper air, and the Gulf of Mexico provides the hot, humid surface air. Under the right conditions, the jet stream acts as a suction and pulls the warm air upward. At the same time, the cold, dry air is forced downward. In the middle of these two drafts, the tornado vortex is created. Unlucky Oklahoma, Texas, and Kansas are the states most likely to be where these two kinds of air streams collide.

The lesson concludes with tornado safety rules in **Handout 49**. Also share school tornado procedures and any additional information from the local Civil Defense Director. Tornadoes normally approach from the southwest. (Another generalization that can be drawn from the map and diagram.) South and west walls are the ones most likely to be penetrated by debris and are also the most likely to collapse. That is why Joe Eagleman's book suggests moving into a northeast room.

MATERIALS:
Handouts 48 and 49, colored pencils

TERMS:
distribution, generalization, jet stream, tornado, vortex

Resources

1. Easleman, Joe R. *Severe and Unusual Weather.* New York: Van Nostrand Reinhold & Company, 1983.

2. Lane, Frank W. *The Elements Rage.* New York: Chilton Books, 1965.

Procedure

1. Ask students if they can guess which states have the most tornadoes. Answers will vary. List their responses on the chalkboard. Have the class rank order the listing.

2. Have students compare their rank order with the information provided on **Handout 48**. Ask which state had the most tornadoes. (Texas, 118) The fewest? (Alaska and Rhode Island had none.) Their state? (Answers will vary depending on location.) Locate these states on a U.S. wall map.

3. For classwork or homework, have students locate each state and transfer the chart's tornado statistics to the map on **Handout 48**. Exchange numbered maps and do a peer check for accuracy. Review the legend and have students use colored pencils to color-code the legend. Guided by the numbers they have written, ask students to color-code their maps according to the legend. Display the completed maps for ready reference.

Suggested Responses, Handout 48:

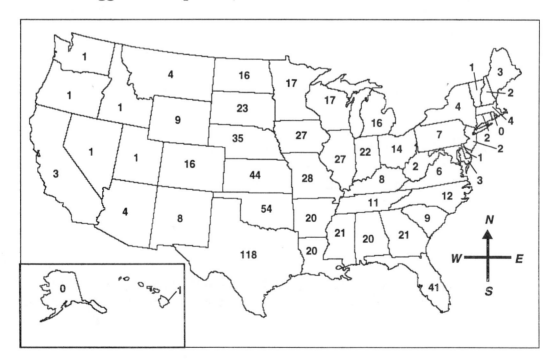

[1] Adapted from *Merrill Social Studies: Outline Map Resource Book* (Columbus, Ohio: Charles E. Merrill Publishing Company, 1986), 6.

4. The completed maps illustrate tornado patterns. Remind students that the patterns provide the basis for making generalizations. Review the criteria for generalizations;
   1. A generalization is a true statement.
   2. A generalization summarizes a lot of data.
   3. Insights are provided by generalizations.

5. Use the displayed maps and the sample on **Handout 48**, page 4 to model how to draw generalizations from the information. Allow a few minutes for students, individually or in pairs, to draw and record four generalizations. Share and discuss their answers. Review correct responses.
   Suggested Responses, Handout 48:
   Answers will vary but might include such generalizations as
   1. *Most tornadoes occur in the south central part of the United States.*
   2. *There are few tornadoes in the Western Mountain states.*
   3. *There are few tornadoes in the Northeast.*
   4. *The farther from the Great Plains states one goes, the less likely one is to experience a tornado.*

6. Conduct a discussion which helps students understand *why* the tornado pattern exists. Share information from Notes to the Teacher.

7. If tornadoes occur locally, distribute **Handout 49** and review tornado safety rules with students.

Enrichment/Extension

1. Conduct a poster contest. Have students make posters relative to tornado safety rules. Award prizes and display all posters.

2. Replicate the activity using other content with which students can prepare maps and draw generalizations. Good maps to use can include ones on population density, average income, or the incidence of hurricanes or earthquakes. Consider using content that includes other countries to provide a global context.

Name _____

Date _____

Tornado Statistics

Name of State	Annual Number
Alabama	20
Alaska	0
Arizona	4
Arkansas	20
California	3
Colorado	16
Connecticut	2
Delaware	1
Florida	41
Georgia	21
Hawaii	1
Idaho	1
Illinois	27
Indiana	22
Iowa	27
Kansas	44
Kentucky	8
Louisiana	20
Maine	3
Maryland	3
Massachusetts	4
Michigan	16
Minnesota	17
Mississippi	21
Missouri	28
Montana	4
Nebraska	35
Nevada	1
New Hampshire	2

© COPYRIGHT, The Center for Learning. Used with permission. Not for resale.

Name _____

Date _____

New Jersey	2
New Mexico	8
New York	4
North Carolina	12
North Dakota	16
Ohio	14
Oklahoma	54
Oregon	1
Pennsylvania	7
Rhode Island	0
South Carolina	9
South Dakota	23
Tennessee	11
Texas	118
Utah	1
Vermont	1
Virginia	6
Washington	1
West Virginia	2
Wisconsin	17
Wyoming	9 [1]

[1] U.S. Department of Commerce, *Climatological Data*, Vol. 30, No. 1, Jan. 1979. (Washington, D.C.: Government Printing Office), 65.

© COPYRIGHT, The Center for Learning. Used with permission. Not for resale.

Social Studies Activities
U.S. History and Geography 1
Lesson 20
Handout 48 (page 3)

Name _____

Date _____

Tornadoes and the States

2

LEGEND

Avg. number of
tornadoes per year

0–15 ☐

16–30 ☐

31–45 ☐

46
and up ☐

² Adapted from *Merrill Social Studies: Outline Map Resource Book* (Columbus, Ohio: Charles E. Merrill Publishing Company, 1986), 6.

© COPYRIGHT, The Center for Learning. Used with permission. Not for resale.

Social Studies Activities
U.S. History and Geography 1
Lesson 20
Handout 48 (page 4)

Name _____

Date _____

Generalizations About Tornadoes

Sample: There are very few on the West Coast.

1. _____

2. _____

3. _____

4. _____

Tornadoes and the Jet Stream

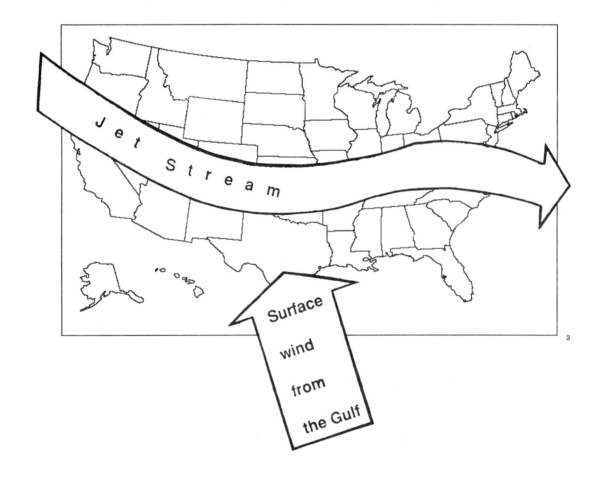

[3] Joe R. Eagleman, *Severe and Unusual Weather* (New York: Van Nostrand Reinhold Company, 1983), 105.

© COPYRIGHT, The Center for Learning. Used with permission. Not for resale.

Name _____

Date _____

Tornado Safety Rules

If you can, . . .   go to an underground concrete shelter or a reinforced concrete basement.

If you can't move underground, . . .   move to a room on the northeast side of a building.

If you're in open country . . .   move at right angles to the tornado.

If you can't get away from it . . .   lie in a ditch or ravine.

*Don't seek protection in a car.

*Don't seek protection in a mobile home.

[4] Ibid., 111–112.

© COPYRIGHT, The Center for Learning. Used with permission. Not for resale.

Acknowledgments

For permission to reprint all works in this volume by each of the following authors, grateful acknowledgment is made to the holders of copyright, publishers, or representatives named below.

Lesson 2, Handout 9

Excerpts from *Familiar Quotations,* John Bartlett, edited by Emily Morison Beck, 1980. Published by Little, Brown & Co., Boston, Massachusetts.

Lessons 4, 18, Handouts 13, 44

Map of the United States from *Merrill Social Studies: Outline Map Resource Book*, 1986. Copyright 1986 by Merrill Publishing Company, Division of Bell & Howell Co., Columbus, Ohio. Reprinted with permission.

Lesson 7, Handout 19

Excerpts from *Home and Child Life in Colonial Days* by Shirley Glubok. Reprinted with permission of Macmillan Publishing Company. Text, Copyright © 1969 by Shirley Glubok Tamarin.

Lesson 9, Handout 23

Two commemorative stamps, "Opening of the Erie Canal" and "Benjamin Banneker, 1980 Commemorative Issue No. 3" from *The Postal Service Guide to U.S. Stamps*, 15th Edition, 1988. Copyright © United States Postal Service. Reprinted with permission.

Lesson 11

Excerpt from *The New Oxford Companion to Music*, Denis Arnold, General Editor, 1983. Published by Oxford University Press, Oxford, England.

Lesson 11, Handout 27

Excerpt from *From Slave to Statesman: The Life and Times of Frederick Douglass*, by Frederick Douglass, abridged by Glenn Munson, 1972. Published by Noble Book Press, New York, New York.

Lesson 11, Handout 27

Lyrics from "Go Down Moses" from *The Fireside Book of Folk Songs* by Margaret Bradford Boni. Copyright © 1947, 1974 by Simon & Schuster, Inc., and Artists and Writers Guild, Inc. Reprinted by permission of Simon & Schuster, Inc.

Lesson 12, Handout 29

Excerpts from *Funk & Wagnalls Standard Dictionary of the English Language*, 1965, Vol. I and Vol. II. Published by J.G. Ferguson Publishing Co., Chicago, Illinois.

Lesson 12, Handout 30

Excerpt from *Our Names: Where They Came from and What They Mean* by Eloise Lambert and Mario Pei, 1960. Copyright Lothrop, Lee & Shepard Books, a Division of William Morrow & Co., New York, New York. Reprinted with permission.

Lesson 13

Excerpt from *The Oxford Dictionary of Quotations*, 1980. Published by Oxford University Press, Oxford, England.

Lesson 13, Handout 33

Poem, "Truth and Love" from *McGuffey Reader Update*, Homesite Edition by Milton R. Revzin. Published 1975 by Scott Press, Youngstown, Ohio.

Lesson 14, Handout 35

Excerpt from *The Collected Works of Abraham Lincoln*, edited by Roy P. Basler. Copyright © 1953 by The Abraham Lincoln Association. Reprinted by permission of Rutgers University Press.

Lesson 14, Handout 35

Excerpt from *Dictionary of American Biography* by Dumas Malone, 1933. Reprinted by permission of American Council of Learned Societies, New York, New York.

Lesson 16, Handout 39

Adaptation of map of Washington, D.C. taken from *World Geography Workbook* by Herbert H. Gross, 1986. Published by Allyn & Bacon, Needham Heights, Massachusetts.

Lesson 19, Handout 46

Statistics from *The Times World Weather Guide*. Copyright © 1984 by E.A. Pearce and C.G. Smith. Reprinted by permission of Times Books, a division of Random House, Inc.

Lesson 20, Handouts 48, 49

Excerpts from *Severe and Unusual Weather*, 2nd edition, Joe R. Eagleman, 1990, Trimedia Publishing Co., Lenexa, Kansas.

Social Studies Series

Advanced Placement

Advanced Placement U.S. History, Book 1
Advanced Placement U.S. History, Book 1, Student Edition
Advanced Placement U.S. History, Book 2
Advanced Placement U.S. History, Book 2, Student Edition
Advanced Placement Economics
Advanced Placement European History, Book 1
Advanced Placement European History, Book 1, Student Edition
Advanced Placement European History, Book 2
Advanced Placement European History, Book 2, Student Edition
Advanced Placement U.S. Government and Politics
Advanced Placement U.S. Government and Politics, Student Edition

Basic Skills

Basic Skills, Geography
Basic Skills, Government
Basic Skills, United States History
Basic Skills, World Cultures/World History

Economics

Economics, Book 1: Microeconomics and the American Economy
Economics, Book 2: Macroeconomics and the American Economy

Government

U.S. Government, Book 1: We, the People
U.S. Government, Book 2: Government of the People and by the People

Intermediate Social Studies

Ohio History and Geography
U. S. History and Geography, Book 1: Beginning–1877
U. S. History and Geography, Book 2: 1878–Present
World History and Geography, Book 1: The East
World History and Geography, Book 2: The West

Issues

American Social Issues
Contemporary Issues
Current Issues in Global Education
Issues in Our Changing World

Junior High

U. S. History, Book 1: Beginning–1876
U. S. History, Book 2: 1876–Present
World Cultures and Geography

United States History

U. S. History, Book 1: Beginning–1865
U. S. History, Book 2: 1866–1920
U. S. History, Book 3: 1920–1960
U. S. History, Book 4: 1960–1990

World History

World History, Book 1: Beginning–1200 A.D.
World History, Book 2: 1201–1814
World History, Book 3: 1815–1919
World History, Book 4: 1920–1992

The Center for Learning

The Publisher

All instructional materials identified by the TAP® (Teachers/ Authors/Publishers) trademark are developed by a national network of teachers whose collective educational experience distinguishes the publishing objective of The Center for Learning, a non-profit educational corporation founded in 1970.

Concentrating on values-related disciplines, The Center publishes humanities and religion curriculum units for use in public and private schools and other educational settings. Approximately 400 language arts, social studies, novel/drama, life issues, and faith publications are available.

While acutely aware of the challenges and uncertain solutions to growing educational problems, The Center is committed to quality curriculum development and to the expansion of learning opportunities for all students. Publications are regularly evaluated and updated to meet the changing and diverse needs of teachers and students. Teachers may offer suggestions for development of new publications or revisions of existing titles by contacting

The Center for Learning

Administrative/Editorial Office
21590 Center Ridge Road
Rocky River, Ohio, 44116
(440) 331-1404 • FAX (440) 331-5414
Email: cfl@stratos.net
Web: http://www.centerforlearning.org

For a free catalog containing order and price information and a descriptive listing of titles, contact

The Center for Learning

Shipping/Business Office
P.O. Box 910
Villa Maria, PA 16155
(724) 964-8083 • (800) 767-9090
FAX (888) 767-8080